I0021625

HOW HACKERS CAN CRUSH YOUR BUSINESS

Why Most Businesses Don't Have A Clue About Cybersecurity Or What To Do About It.

Learn the latest cyber security, compliance, laws and risk management solutions.

Craig A. Petronella

Published by

Petronella Technology Group, Inc., Raleigh, North Carolina

Craig Petronella, Raleigh, North Carolina's top cyber security expert and IT authority, has authored multiple books, including *Peace of Mind Computer Support.* He has spent 30 years advising clients and protecting computer information. Craig makes sure your medical practice network works when you need it the most, and is a celebrity in his field and hometown.

Craig is frequently quoted in the local Raleigh news and appears on local TV news for his expertise in protecting local businesses and medical practice owners from hackers halfway around the world in places such as the Ukraine, Russia, and China. Petronella has been quoted and featured on NBC News, CBS North Carolina, ABC 11, Raleigh & Charlotte, NC Time Warner Cable News, WNCN TV (local Raleigh TV), PRNews Wire, and Newsobserver.com.

Table of Contents

Section One - Accountability
Chapter 1 -- Small Businesses are Under Attack: A Guide to
Protecting Yourself from the World of Cyber Threats
Chapter 2 -- A Breach of Confidentiality Can Be Hazardous to Your
Health
Chapter 3 -- Don't Make Clients and Partners Look at You Sideways

Section Two - Information Theft Devices
Chapter 4 -- Keyloggers
Chapter 5 -- Web Scraping
Chapter 6 -- Backdoors

Section Three – Malware
Chapter 7 -- Botnet
Chapter 8 -- Data corruption
Chapter 9 -- Ransomware

Section Four - Defending Data and Devices
Chapter 10 -- Steps Anyone Can Take to Defend Themselves
Chapter 11 -- Importance of Keeping Ahead of Hackers
Chapter 12 -- Choosing an IT Provider for Cyber Security

Four Pillars of IT Success Analysis

Appendix

SECTION ONE - ACCOUNTABILITY

Most small businesses close their doors after just a couple of years.

That was a fact even before the Internet complicated things. Now there are even more threats to the small business owner than there were before. You can lose access to the systems on which you depend. You can get hacked and cleaned out by some unscrupulous nerd. You can even unintentionally compromise your customers' credit information, a mistake that comes with stiff penalties, both from the folks who allow you to accept credit cards in the first place and from the customers whose confidence you've lost.

It's enough to scare anybody (or at least, it should be), because the dangers are real. So real, in fact, that the government has started to get in on the action. They've laid out legislation and standards and requirements, hoops for businesses to jump through in order to comply. And the consequences of failing to do so? Well, assuming you dodge the jail time that's possible with some particular issues, you better believe there are fines just waiting to slap you in the face.

All of these problems are peculiar to the digital age, making it harder than ever to stay in business. This isn't to say that technology doesn't come with its benefits, of course. Being able to accept credit cards, being able to quickly access customer information, inventory, bank account information, and even cloud accounting have all made it easier to do business. What is harder is doing business SAFELY. Because along with the conveniences of modern technology, there come a myriad ways that things can go wrong.

There are some issues that are specific to one industry or another and the businesses that work with them. For example, health records are surprisingly valuable on the black market. Uncle Sam has put several standards in place to protect patient information, but those standards apply to more than just doctors' offices and hospitals. Any business that works with medical providers is responsible for meeting the same strict requirements, lest they compromise valuable information and expose innocent people to identity theft and other consequences. Between the government fines and the possible time in prison, A HIPAA violation spells almost certain doom for a small business.

And what about credit cards? If you want to be able to continue offering this practically necessary convenience to your customers, you have to be able to protect their information. Many of the big name cards (Visa, MasterCard, etc.) have their own set of standards you must live up to if you want to accept their cards. If you fail the test, they won't do business with you. In turn, customers who depend on the use of these cards won't do business with you, either. And before you know it, you're insolvent.

Bottom line, what we're trying to say here is that the security of your digital data is so valuable that its importance can't be exaggerated. The life of your business depends on it.

So what exactly do you need to do to protect yourself, your business, and your customers? Glad you asked. This book is designed to tell you exactly that. We'll take a look at some of the more egregious mistakes you can make, the scariest pitfalls in front of you, and how you can dodge the bad guys.

Let's get down to business.

Chapter 1 -- Small Businesses are Under Attack: A Guide to Protecting Yourself from the World of Cyber Threats

I have no idea what the statistics are and frankly, I don't need to know; the numbers are constantly changing anyway. What I do know is that there are loads of small businesses in this country. And unless you're some off-the-grid enthusiast that sells rare coins in a brick and mortar shop with a register till dating back to the fall of Rome, chances are that your business relies on the Internet in some form or fashion. Odds are, unless you're clinging to the absurd hope that there will be a resurgence of the Pony Express, most of your transactions and correspondence are handled digitally.

America boasts a vibrant small business economy. Roughly half the nation is employed by small businesses. And while the definition of "small business" varies, let's just keep it simple for this publication, since the topics we're covering can get somewhat complicated in themselves. Life is hard enough, right? Anyway, for our purposes, a small business is any corporation, partnership, or sole proprietorship that employs fewer than 500 people.

To simplify even more, ask yourself this question: As the owner of a small business, can you afford to employ, insure, and maintain an entire division within your organization solely for the purposes of cyber security? Chances are you cannot. And truth be told, there's no reason you should.

Cyber security requires vigilance and expertise, which essentially calls for a robust budget allotted for gadgets and training so your crew of experts will be prepared to repel the relentless invaders. Computer criminals are out there, they're hungry, and they're hoping to find vulnerabilities someplace lucrative. They could very well find what they're looking for in your business.

I've heard all the excuses.

My small business is tiny... no one notices us.

We've got nothing to steal.

Why would cyber crooks come after my business when there are plenty of others to target?

Let's address this nonsense. Because if that's your line of thinking, you're in for a serious gut punch, and it won't just be from hackers –

whether they're members of an Eastern European syndicate, a former employee holding a grudge, or a soon-to-be former employee that's about to do something stupid or cruel. You could very well find yourself in some serious trouble with the government.

Because you're right about one thing... you are too small. You're small enough that the government has little compunction about participating in that gut punch should you be found out of compliance with their standards of security. Until you grow your business enough to wield some clout or you've acquired a sister-in-law serving in Congress, there isn't much you can do to avoid the wrath of government.

And it may seem counterintuitive to you, but small businesses are prime targets. Hacking and cyber crime are so prevalent and efficient that experienced criminals can bleed dry several small businesses before they break for lunch, tea, siesta, or vodka (depending on where they're from and what floats their boat). And the reason you're not *too* small is because anyone in business is in the scopes. Think about the resources the mega-players in any industry have in place to prevent attacks and mitigate risk. Yet they still can't get it right. Remember Sony? And to be honest, that particular hack wasn't all that complicated. This begs the question, what is your exposure?

Remember this: When the predators attack, oftentimes all you have to do is outrun the slowest in the herd. So don't be the slowest in the herd.

First things first. Before we even worry about how the hackers will get you, we'll dive into your liability. As we mentioned before, the government has taken an interest in ensuring that consumers are adequately protected. Billions of dollars are lost each year in digital fraud and theft, and as you can imagine, industries are tired of paying out recoupment costs. Naturally, they look to the government to do something about it. Often times these attempts at establishing some sort of order blankets all businesses, including your small enterprise.

Does your business accept credit and debit cards? Of course it does. We're in the 21st century, for Pete's sake. This means you're liable for all kinds of personal information each time a customer or client forks over a credit card or credit information to do business with you. Are you familiar with the legislation in place that requires businesses to take precautions with that credit information? Because it's there, you know.

Initially this legislation was designed to hold larger corporations responsible. However, it's imperative to understand that the Big Guys are no longer the sole targets. Both the government and the hackers realize this. You need to as well. Criminals don't really give a shake where they steal information from, aside from the level of ease in getting what they want and the risk of getting busted. Cyber crime is so prevalent that even the government has caught on that *everyone* needs to be held accountable. You are part of "everyone."

It's important to understand some of the origins of our current business and financial dynamics, so let's go over some history for a bit. Thanks to the dawn of the Digital Age, business models have radically changed. Information is no longer stored under lock and key or shredded and then that's the end of it. Now everything's out there in the cloud. Legislation has hardly kept up with the technological leaps, but when it does take a stab at addressing the problems that come with those leaps, their attempts are often sweeping strokes with unintended consequences.

In 1999, Bill Clinton signed into law the Gramm-Leach-Bliley Act (GLBA). Some of you may have heard about the Glass-Steagall Act, which was repealed during his administration, and which many attribute as one of the root causes of the 2008 financial crisis. GLBA was the bill that repealed Glass-Steagall to allow for investment banking firms and commercial banking firms to exist under the same roof.

Aside from the banking crisis that followed, what this meant for our purposes was the glut of information consolidated into one place. Part of this bill required that these firms demonstrate adequate and competent preventative measures to protect their customers' information. As you can imagine, hacking into Citigroup (or any of the other big banks) would've been one doozy of a score. The institutions not only had customer account numbers and information, but the account information for private and municipal pension funds. Oh, what glorious goodies they had packaged for any hacker to access and exploit.

The privacy notice clause in the bill, which by today's standards is a bit basic, requires institutions to explain the types of information they gather from their clients as well as how it will be shared and for what purposes. This is part of the ocean of fine print they hand you absolutely every time you do absolutely anything. These institutions also need a written plan in accordance with The Safeguard Rule that explains their measures and procedures to prevent breaches and must detail how they will respond should it occur. This law, while still in effect and enforceable, is primitive after less than twenty years on the books. Also, it's key to remember that it's aimed at you, the business owner. It's a deterrent designed to make sure all of your whatnot is wired tight.

One of the bits and pieces of GLBA was the Safeguards Rule that applies to all IT systems. What it basically says is that if you house private or non-public information, you have to protect it, and you have to protect it to certain standards. Several federal laws have since been founded on the back of the Safeguards Rule, which has given rise to the Service Organization Controls (SOC). Auditors of IT systems use SOC to determine the adequacy of your data protection. There are three types of auditing procedures: SOC 1, SOC 2, and SOC 3. Certifications for SOC 2 Type 2 enable your business to exchange data with other certified IT systems, so it's necessary in order to connect with other businesses.

In 2004, the major credit card companies took matters into their own hands and established The Payment Card Industry Data Security Standard (PCI-DSS). This is one of those nifty little instances of the free market actually policing itself. Granted, the big banks were financially motivated as they covered a mountain of fraud charges and such, so they imposed their own standards on merchants who want to do business with them. You're probably aware of these standards, assuming you accept credit cards. If you're one of those "cash only" enterprises, you're probably not reading this and are probably hiding from the authorities.

These standards have been revised over the years, but they do cover these barebones basics:

- Install and maintain a secured network.

- Arrange protection for credit card storage and encrypted transmissions over public networks, etc.

- Regularly update anti-virus software protection.

- Regularly monitor and test the networks.

- Maintain an information security policy.

As the business owner, you need to be aware of a couple things. It may seem a well-intended policy implemented by the Biggies to ensure that consumer information is all protected and safe. Wouldn't that be nice? However, keep in mind that these institutions can make their own assessments and fine merchants if they are found wanting after a breach. You know what fines mean to a private enterprise? Loss for you and profit for them. Just like banks love to inflict those overdraft fees on the working poor, they also view your incompetence or ignorance as a profit center.

All of this means that you now have someone else looking to pick your pockets. And these are supposed to be your partners in doing business. If we cast our faith in humanity aside for a moment, it isn't difficult to imagine teams of malcontented trolls locked away somewhere auditing merchants for the sole purpose of finding excuses to fine them and increase shareholder profit. This is private enterprise motivation. You can bank on their enthusiasm for searching out any and all ways in which you mucked up.

You'll notice that we haven't even gotten to the hackers yet, the criminals that you expected all of this to be about.

In 2003, the Bush administration signed into law the Fair and Accurate Credit Transactions Act (FACTA). This was essentially an amendment to the Fair Credit Reporting Act of 1970. The main purpose of the law was to grant consumers the right to view their credit history once a year from all the major credit agencies. For our purposes, we'll consider the provision that allows consumers to report identity theft or suspicious activity that they feel will lead to some kind of foul play.

Also, businesses are required to safely dispose of sensitive information. This means shredding or destroying documents with personal information, or as in one real-world case, not leaving patient prescription information in the dumpster for anyone to find and use. (Gift wrap it for the identity thieves, why don't you. Sheesh.)

It was with this law that credit card receipts and slips were shortened so they only revealed five or six digits of account numbers. Today that seems like a pretty obvious method of protection, but not so long ago it wasn't the way of things. Think about that. What are we currently doing as a business community that will seem like insane and self-destructive negligence in a just a few years, perhaps as little as a few months?

The point here isn't to scare the stuffing out of you so much as to drive home the point that you shouldn't be the one assessing the strengths and weaknesses of your business's digital security. The field of cyber security is an industry, and it's thriving for a reason. There are professionals out there who can navigate these laws and policies to ensure that you don't get reamed from the supposed good guys in the event that you ever suffer a breach. I mean, let's face it; breaches are inevitable. But you can at least prevent most of them and mitigate the ones that do occur. Subsequently, if you demonstrated that you did all you could to prevent these breaches, then you're in the clear as far as Uncle Sam is concerned, and none of the big banks can giggle greedily as they slap you with a fine.

But let's assume for a moment that you're still not convinced it's necessary to take the potency of your cyber security measures seriously. Perhaps you're still willing to risk it. You believe your business is too small to be on the hacker radar, or you're confident that you're doing enough to outrun the slowest buffalo. Okay, then.

Here's what you have to understand, though. The rest of the business world is on the move. As integrated as everything is, business is reacting to the market, and the market is under constant threat from cyber misdeeds. It's increasingly common to encounter standards for protection and protocols when approaching potential clients or associates. The better covered you are in this area, the better you present yourself. Consider the wisdom in showing up prepared, complying with industry standards rather than learning late in the game that you're not eligible for consideration until you've implemented them. What would this say about you and your organization's innovation and competence? How would it impact your reputation? Investing in your cyber wellbeing could be make the difference between closing a deal and not closing a deal.

Chapter 2 -- A Breach of Confidentiality Can Be Hazardous to Your Health

Ever since the U.S. Senate endorsed it in 1996, the Health Insurance Portability and Accountability Act (HIPAA) has set forth the standard for protecting Americans' private health information.

The stakes were further raised in 2009 with the Health Information Technology for Economic and Clinical Health Act (HITECH). This addition would shine the spotlight on the electronic aspect of health information, including the proper handling of electronic personal health information. Basically, it took HIPAA to new heights via computers. HITECH actively promotes the adoption of health information technology, pushing the medical community to get with the 21st century and digitize. The goal is for the nation's health network to become increasingly interconnected.

But it's important to recognize that, in order for computer systems all over the country to communicate with each other this way, an immeasurable amount of work had to go into program planning. Some extraordinarily gifted and experienced programmers stayed busy for a long time. And they aren't done. These IT specialists are now further challenged by cyber attacks and hackers.

HIPAA requires that you take action to counteract such threats, and there are penalties for negligence if you don't. This means that you can suffer the consequences when an information breach occurs against your will or even without your knowledge. The traditional brand of PHI (personal health information) is the stuff that comes in a physical, paper format. That same information in electronic format is referred to as ePHI, or electronic personal health information. It's the data stored on your server and on the technology devices within your organization. Regardless of the format, this information must be completely secure and inaccessible to any and all unauthorized persons.

And what is considered PHI? Anything that directly links an individual to a current, past, or future health condition. If health information has an individual's name, address, date of birth, social security number, or any other such personal identifying data, that information is considered PHI. If your organization processes, stores, transmits, modifies, or in any other way touches protected health information, you're responsible for taking very specific actions that ensure its security and compliance with HIPAA regulations.

There are two major groups that are obligated by law to uphold the HIPAA standards.

The first of these groups are referred to as covered entities. A covered entity (CE) is defined as an organization that creates and originates PHI. There are 700,000 of these covered entities in the United States:

 *Doctors, clinics, psychologists, dentists, chiropractors, nursing homes, pharmacies,
 hospitals, and any other practitioner who initially generates PHI through interaction with a patient.

 *Government programs that pay for health care, such as Medicare and Medicaid, health insurance companies, HMOs, and employer health plans.

 *Health care clearinghouses. These are the organizations that process nonstandard information and convert data from one form to another, turning paper PHI into ePHI.

The other group that must comply with HIPAA rules are called business associates (BA). The 700,000 covered entities do business with millions of business associates.

Business associates manage, transmit, modify, subcontract, or otherwise handle protected information. There are subcontracted companies who do quality assurance reviews, patient satisfaction surveys, companies who work on your server and run cables in your building, companies who pick up and dispose of your shredded records, OSHA reviewers, Medicare auditors, Medicaid auditors, utilization review and process improvement people, accountants, attorneys, and vendors of a wide variety of services. On average, the data generated from one interaction between a health provider and a patient is seen, in whole or in part, by 150 people. ALL of them are legally obligated to protect the PHI of the patient.

For example, let's say you're an accountant who has a doctor as a client. In the course of your work, you are privy to certain portions of patient information. If you have access to information that identifies the patient (social security number, telephone number, street address, date of birth, etc.) and the information also references a current or past health condition, you're on the hook. If PHI is within your grasp, you are within HIPAA's.

The acting HIPAA sheriff for the Department of Health and Human Services is the Office of Civil Rights (OCR). The OCR enforces HIPAA rules, and they have full authority to perform periodic audits to check for compliance. In fact, HITECH specifically requires the OCR to perform these periodic audits, both of covered entities and business associates. If you haven't had one of these audits yet, it's only a matter of time.

The OCR has developed a thorough protocol for systematically assessing the controls and processes that covered entities and business associates have put into place to try and keep PHI secure. If there is anything at all wrong with an organization's handling of PHI, the OCR audit will find it. The fines for failing to comply max out at $50,000. That is per violation. But a business can be slapped with a penalty of up to $1.5 million. This is still not a total of possible fines. The $1.5 million is merely a maximum for the penalty within each incident category. Criminal penalties have no cap whatsoever. If your organization has issues in multiple categories, you can rack up a very serious bill.

And the responsibility to keep up with the changes made to HIPAA and HITECH directives sits squarely on your shoulders. Are you familiar with all of the regulations, principles, and laws that you are expected to follow?

Progress is moving so fast that a whole new industry of cyber security has arisen to service this need. It might behoove you to go a step further and enlist the expertise of an IT security expert, even though you may have an IT department in place. The benefit of an outside consultant may prove the difference between a catastrophic oversight and a simple fix/adjustment of practices already in place.

HITECH HIPAA Violations

Data breaches that involve business associates are far more likely to occur than those involving covered entities. And worse, these breaches tend to involve far more patients when they occur. As the saying goes, "To err is human, but to really mess things up, it takes a computer." That's all too true, all too often. A computer error can expose the protected health information of hundreds, thousands, or even millions of patients in an instant. And a breach in HIPAA policy means penalties, whether that breach results from deliberate maliciousness, blasé negligence, or unintended ignorance. Some examples:

In January 2015, 80 million records were breached as a result of a cyber attack on Anthem. On the same day, Primera, experienced a breach that affected another 11 million records. Together, these two security breaches resulted in the largest theft of medical records ever reported... 91 million patients in just one day.

The fines can be staggering. In June 2012, an un-encrypted hard drive was stolen from a car. The breach affected 501 patients. The fine: $1.7 million.

In July 2013, the PHI of 612,402 patients was available on the Internet to unauthorized users for more than five months. The managed care company had upgraded their software, but had failed to perform an adequate technical evaluation afterward. The fine was $1.7 million.

In April 2014, a laptop computer containing data that had not been properly encrypted was stolen. The PHI of 870 patients was compromised. The fine was $1.73 million.

HIPAA Phase 2 Audits

Beginning in the spring of 2016, Phase 2 of HIPAA kicked off with hundreds of audits. If an office or organization is found to be deficient in security measures and their PHI is at risk, fines can still be charged by the OCR whether a breach of confidential information has occurred or not. Many items on the HIPAA checklist involve HITECH security. You must actively take measures to protect yourself. Unfamiliarity with your HIPAA rules is no excuse for their violation.
Would your organization get a clean bill of health?

 Consider these few examples, a mere sampling from the HIPAA audit checklist:

Have you implemented procedures for terminating access to ePHI when an employee leaves your organization?

Do you have policies and procedures for guarding against, detecting, and reporting malicious software?

Do you have procedures for monitoring login attempts and reporting discrepancies?

Do you have a contingency plan (i.e. policies and procedures) for responding to an emergency such as fire, vandalism, system failure, and natural disasters that could damage systems that contain ePHI?

Have you established (and implemented as needed) procedures to enable continuation of critical business processes and for protection of ePHI while operating in the emergency mode?

Have you implemented a mechanism to encrypt and decrypt ePHI?

Have you implemented technical security measures to guard against unauthorized access to ePHI that is being transmitted over an electronic communications network?

Has a risk analysis been completed annually?

And this doesn't even really scratch the surface of all the nooks and crannies an audit will explore.

In the article "Brace for HIPAA Audits as They Arrive in Early 2016," James E. Bowers reports that "the most common deficiency found by OCR in its pilot audits was an organization's failure to conduct a security risk assessment to identify and mitigate risks to PHI (e.g. PHI on exposed servers, unencrypted laptops, unchanged default passwords, outdated security software, and inadequate training). As hard as it is to believe, many HIPAA entities still have not implemented this 'lesson learned.' On September 2, 2015, OCR announced a $750,000 settlement with Indiana-based Cancer Care Group PC, because it had failed to conduct an enterprise-wide risk analysis and implement follow-on device and media control policies to protect the transportation of un-encrypted

PHI. OCR contends that a risk assessment could have identified the control weakness.

Do your business and organization a favor. Consult a cyber-security expert at your earliest opportunity. Have confidence knowing the ePHI in your computer system is safe and inaccessible. Then, when OCR contacts you for an audit, you can be confident that no HIPAA violations or fines will jeopardize the success of your company.

Chapter 3 -- Don't Make Clients and Partners Look at You Sideways

Let's imagine it's date night. You and your significant other are gearing up to go out and enjoy some much-needed rest, relaxation, and recreation. But before you can hit the road and have a good time, you need to find a quality babysitter to look after your little ones. So you call up a friend of the family who has a teenager who can't wait to earn a few bucks.

When that teenager shows up, you find out that your children would probably be better off by themselves. As soon as you open the door, the kid marches right past you into the living room and switches on the television. You get a half-hearted nod and a wave-off when you deliver your instructions. And when you get halfway down the block and realize you forgot something at your house, you turn around and discover the worst bit of all. Your youngest child is outside alone, playing near the street. And the babysitter is still on the couch, completely oblivious to the fact that this is happening.

How likely are you to hire this babysitter again? Would you even go through with your plans for the night? No. No way. Because you can't trust them to protect what's precious to you.

What would happen if your customers and business partners found out that you were as negligent with their private information as that teenager was with your kiddos? Is there any question in your mind that your business would suffer?

If you're going to accept credit cards, you need to hold the trust of those that do business with you. That includes customers whose credit card information you're accepting, of course, but it also includes suppliers and other companies that partner with you in some way, shape, or form. Fellow business owners want the trust of their own customers, too, and if they think that partnering with you puts their customers at risk, they won't want to touch you with a ten-foot pole. Problems with your cyber security can make you a pariah in more ways than one.

And if you're thinking that, should a breach of your security actually happen, you'll just keep a lid on it and no one will be the wiser, think again. It's your legal responsibility to officially report a data breach if one occurs. These security breach notification laws are on the state level, so we won't go into the specifics here, but it would behoove you to look into what your state requires. But in general, you are obligated to make a written report to customers, clients, suppliers, patients, or whoever else does business with you (a process that is sure to cost you time and money as you go about this public self-shaming). So, yeah. Either people are gonna know about your security failures or you'll be on the wrong side of the law. You choose.

One type of business partnership that is of particular importance regardless of industry is your banking relationship. We've already taken a look at how your bank can punish you financially for falling short of your security responsibilities, but imagine if your bank refused to do business with you at all. How badly would that mess things up for you? I'm guessing pretty badly.

You see, when you violate PCI standards (remember those?), fines don't go straight to your business. They go straight to your bank. And when your bank gets poked in the eye with a fine ranging anywhere from $5,000 to $100,000 for each and every month that you're out of compliance, they're going to take issue with you. They may even stop giving lollipops to your kids when you come in to make a deposit. And while you could always make it up to Junior by buying a lollipop at the corner store on the way home, that corner store ain't gonna step up to the plate when your bank leaves you in the lurch come payday. Employee paychecks are a bit tougher to replace than a missing piece of candy.

But let's say you handle things as soon as humanly possible and get yourself in compliance so that your bank decides not to break up with you after all. How are your customers going to feel about the fact that you dropped the ball in the first place? I'll put it this way… Target. Remember what happened with them? Of course, you do. After all, they jeopardized the private information of 48 million people, leading to Senators demanding investigations and the pain of class-action lawsuits. And then there's the fact that you do, in fact, remember all of this. Even if you're cool handing over your plastic to the Target cashier, not everybody feels that way. Target lost existing customers and potential customers alike.

Another potential client or customer that you should consider is the government. The Department of Defense uses the agency supplement of the Defense Federal Acquisition Regulation Supplement (DFARS) to make sure everything is secure. If you have any desire to cash in as a government contractor, you have to be up to their standards with security, including cyber security. NIST 800-171 lays out a set of expectations that align with NIST 800-53, which is the standard for U.S. government cyber security controls. Unless your security is up to snuff in managing and protecting all Controlled Unclassified Information (CUI), you absolutely will not land that contract. Say goodbye to those government dollars.

Speaking of government, in 2002 we got the Sarbanes-Oxley Act (SOX). This is a U.S. federal law that protects shareholders and the general public from accounting errors and fraudulent practices. That's all well and good. What's new, though, is an amendment put before the House of Representatives in 2016 that requires any issuer of securities to specifically state whether or not they have a cyber security expert on their audit committee. This means that if you don't have a cyber security expert in your midst, you're forced to reveal that fact to the public, meaning that not only that you make yourself look bad to consumers, but you also announce to the hacking world that you're susceptible to attack. You invite crooks instead of customers.

Protenus, a company that specializes in healthcare data privacy, released a report that looked closely at just how much cybercrime costs the healthcare industry. The numbers are staggering. The report says that your average healthcare provider suffers to the tune of $5.7 million in lost business. Why? Because 54% of respondents say that they would change doctors in the case of a data breach.

Now just think about this for a second. If a patient trusts his doctor so much that he's willing to stand still while that doctor approaches him with a rubber glove, but he doesn't trust the doctor after a failure to protect private information, how confident are you that customers will stick with you after a breach?

If your customers wouldn't even trust you to come at them with the rubber glove, you have your answer right there.

So, what can you do to inspire confidence and trust in your customers and business partners? Well, aside from the all-important step of avoiding breaches that put you in the spotlight in a bad way, you can (and should) pursue ISO 27001 certification. Getting ISO 27001 certification involves an independent verification that your information security program lives up to an international standard. It also identifies information that could be subject to data laws and sets you up with a risk-based approach to keeping threats to your business under control.

Meeting ISO 27001 standards isn't just a feather in your cap. It's a requirement to do business with some types of customers, a concept we touched on just a few paragraphs ago and earlier in this book. Having ISO 27001 certification lays the foundation for the compliance efforts you need to put forth to get right for PCI, HIPAA, SOX, and so on.

SECTION TWO – INFORMATION THEFT DEVICES

When people conjure up an image of a hacker stealing from them, there are many clichés that come to mind. In the 1990s, Sandra Bullock starred in *The Net.* In this movie, hackers took her identity and altered police computers so that the authorities would think she was a criminal. This isn't likely to happen to you. In fact, chances are that if you have been hacked, you don't even know it. Your information was probably stolen and sold without you having a clue. This begs the question: If they hack into your information and then leave without you catching on, did they actually get anything? The answer is a resounding yes.

Research has shown that there are clear patterns to what hackers may take from you and how they make money off it. There is a direct correlation between how they get into your accounts and what they are after. Often, from your point of view, a hack might start and stop with you getting a phone call from the bank to verify that some transaction was not actually you. They lock certain account information, possibly send you a new bank card, and your life goes on. In more extreme cases, you may try to log into your computer to discover that you are the victim of ransomware, which will lock you out of your hard drive until you pay a fee to re-access your files (or else you may begin receiving little pieces of them in your email).

The largest thefts tend to be passwords and account information, which are then sold on the deep dark web through websites like The Real Deal. Even MySpace account information is sold in bulk on this site. (Side note: I just checked the MySpace site, and it does, in fact, still exist, despite Facebook's best efforts.) This isn't some made-up "black market" from the latest B movie; it is a very real marketplace. The individuals buying this information don't want to be public about obtaining the necessary data, so it is hard to say exactly who is buying it and what they do with it.

What we do know is that this information is often purchased by groups who want access to not one but all of your accounts. They seek bulk buys, including people using just one password for multiple sites. One of the most common uses of this information is spamming. They are then able to approach you or members of your contact list by posing as you and requesting more information or even money. They can send out massive spam emails or messages to the people they originally got the information from by targeting keywords or interests to convince you that they are a legitimate business. Then they can place ransomware or other malware onto your computer.

In this section, we will go through some of the devices and skills used by hackers to get to your information and what they do with it once it is obtained. There is no one answer or solution to protecting yourself. Using the web itself is complicated, as are the ways in which hackers infiltrate your system. We will attempt to break down these complications so that you are better armed to protect yourself, or at the very least, be prepared to respond appropriately if you are hacked.

Chapter 4 -- Keyloggers

Keyloggers are a type of surveillance software. This can also be referred to as software or spyware, but the purpose is the same. Keyloggers have the capability to record every keystroke you make to a log file, and it is usually encrypted. Sometimes referred to as keystroke logger, keyloggers, or system monitors, it is a hardware or software device. We will mostly be discussing the software in this section, but it's important to note that they can also be hardware.

The hardware version is often a small battery-sized plug that serves as a connector between the user's keyboard and the computer. Because the device is designed to look like an ordinary keyboard plug, it's all too easy for someone who wants to monitor your behavior to physically hide right in front of you. If your keyboard plug is in the back of your computer, it's that much easier to hide this device because, let's face it, how often do you check the plug in the back of your system for your keyboard? As you type, the device collects each keystroke and saves it into a text file that's easy to read and stays on its own internal hard drive until the hacker is ready to open, download, and review. However, this means they must physically retrieve the device, making this method less likely to be used by professional hackers looking to gather information from distant locations.

Let's make sure we haven't lost you already by taking a step back to define a couple of key terms. Keep in mind that a log file is a file that lists actions that have happened. A good example is to look at most web services, which maintain a log file listing for every request made to the server. Using log file analysis tools, it's possible to get a strong overview of where visitors are coming from, how they navigate the site, and how often they return. This is where you will note a very familiar term – cookies. Before you get excited and start pouring yourself a glass of milk, it should be noted that these cookies are "online only" and are designed to enable a Webmaster to log even more information about how visitors are accessing the site.

"Encrypted" is another term we will use frequently. Encryption is the translation of data into a secret code that can only be read using a key (think back on the decoder rings they used to hide in breakfast cereal). It's the most effective way to achieve data security, and there is more than one kind of encryption. Once a key is applied to the ciphertext, the information is read as a simple plain text. A Webmaster or hacker might pull all the information they want from a log file, but without a key to decrypt the information, they won't be able to make sense of the cipher text. The two most common types of encryption are asymmetric encryption (a.k.a. public-key encryption) and symmetric encryption.

The software version of keyloggers is designed to avoid the physical interaction between hacker and computer. It's often downloaded unwittingly through spyware and executed as part of a rootkit or Remote Access Trojan (RAT). A rootkit is a set of software tools that enable an unauthorized user to gain access and control of a computer system without being detected. A RAT is roughly the same thing. A keyword is often used to differentiate between legal remote access software (such as what you would use to access your work computer from home) from a hacker gaining illegal access to systems. A keylogger program is typically made up of two different files installed in the same directory. One will be a Dynamic Link Library file (DLL), which will do the recording. The other will be an executable file (.EXE) that installs the DLL file and tells it to start working. The keylogger program will then record each keystroke the user types and upload the data through the Internet. This is the most likely way for a faceless hacker to gain access. The hardware version is for someone much closer to home.

Keyloggers can record all types of information from different sources. They can grab instant messages, emails, and literally anything you type at any time and dump it into a log file. This transforms your keyboard into a spy, spilling the beans on who you are, where you are, what you have, and where your interests lie. Some keylogger programs will record any email addresses you use, website URLs you visit, or keywords you search on a regular basis. The log file can then pass to a specific receiver. Once set up, the work is done for the hacker. He goes to his kitchen to nuke a Hot Pocket as your keyboard merrily does the rest for him, automatically spying on you and sending him your information.

This does not mean that only faceless hackers or the "bad guys" use keyloggers. They can also be used by employers to keep an eye on their employees. If your boss wants to make sure that you're using your computer for work purposes only, they can use keyloggers to track what you are doing. This maintains employee privacy by not looking at the actual details of what they're doing, but simply verifying whether what they type is or is not work related. Some employers use a keylogger to track a variety of items and collect more than just the basics. If designed correctly, they can easily dig into the specifics of their employees' work-time computer use.

Keyloggers can also be embedded in or with spyware, which can transmit your information to a third party without you or the company even knowing it. This all comes down to the creator of the keylogger. There are other ways to use keyloggers, based on the desires of the person using it.

In recent years, there has been a growth in keylogger use on a personal level. That is, your significant other can use a keylogger to keep an eye on you. The hacker harvesting your information doesn't necessarily have to be a nerdy guy living in his mother's basement. Nor does it have to be a Russian group in a bunker somewhere gathering information on foreign powers. The hacker could very well be your spouse, paranoid about what you're doing when you're away from home.

Keyloggers are common, and they're simple enough that your average Joe can set one up after viewing an online tutorial. If your technology-averse mother can conquer eBay, this too is within the realm of possibility. This is one of many reasons why it's a smart idea for you to educate yourself about the tools of a hacker. This information is readily available to everyone, including your family members. We won't delve into the sticky subject of what you may be doing to drive your loved ones to spy on you, but we will break down some of the basics on how they may be going about it.

First, they must gain access to your system. There are many ways to do this, including simply sitting down at your computer after you've finished (but before your system goes to sleep and locks them out). Some trusting people choose not to have a password on their computer, or they allow others to use it. In any case, there are lots of remote access software options available and many other ways for people to gain entry into your system, even if you never share your password with anyone and guard your computer with all sorts of booby traps.

Once they're granted access, the rest is as simple as a Google search. For example, Metasploit's Meterpreter (say that ten times fast) is an uncomplicated site with lots of online forums and tutorials. Once into your system, the hacker can go through and pick what information or software he wants to track, including what URLs you access and what instant messenger chats you have.

Keyloggers are often demonized, but they're also promoted and created with the best of intentions, such as parental monitoring. Concerned parents monitoring their children's use of the Internet are technically hackers using the same techniques as the ones you hear about on the news. They're commonly just using a system purchased at the local Office Max or Staples rather than a more complicated software.

Many groups use this technology for the greater good. Law enforcement officers most certainly use it, and depending on how high in the government you go, it may or may not become more common in the future. In short, keyloggers are not only used for illegal purposes.

The use of keyloggers is a huge debate among privacy advocates, as the potential for abuse is so great. Legislation is always being discussed, passed, or argued over to find ways to make sure that illegal or unauthorized use of keyloggers is a criminal offense.

We aren't here for a political or moral debate; that's something you can take up with your spouse when you find a keylogger device plugged into your home computer. However, it is important to understand that, ultimately, keyloggers are only restricted by a hacker's aptitude for computers.

Chapter 5 -- Web Scraping

Web scraping can also be referred to as screen scraping, web data extraction, and web harvesting. Basically, this technique is the extraction of large amounts of data from a website. The data is then saved to a local file on your computer, database, or server in a table format (a spreadsheet). This is a form of hacking that dramatically affects companies such as Amazon and other large website services. It isn't likely that anyone will use it on your personal site featuring knitting techniques or the best in cat videos from YouTube. However, YouTube itself is most certainly at threat of being scraped.

One of the main differences between web scraping and keyloggers is that scraping is focused primarily on websites and gathering information into a spreadsheet format rather than plain text. The easiest way to understand a tactic like this is to first look at its most common use.

New businesses are the most common culprits using this technique, as they have the most to gain from it. Imagine you're a new company in a pre-existing industry. Your competitors may have already been around for a long time, and they most likely have a stronger client base and more capital with which to work. You decide to implement web scraping to access as much information as you can on your competitors. You're looking for ways to make your product not just competitive but actively better. You look at what the public wants and read about their most common complaints regarding your competitors' product. You research how often they buy said product and how often they feel like they are overpaying for the product. The useful information you can obtain to gain an edge on your competitor becomes endless.

The question of legality now comes into play. Like most things involving the Internet and technology, there isn't one simple answer. Starting in the 1990s, web scraping was mostly seen as a nuisance to a website, but it was not viewed as a hindrance, so it wasn't prohibited. Since it didn't get in the way of the website's ability to do business, it wasn't really addressed, and for the most part, scrapers went unpunished. The individual website just had to deal with the fact that their information was being scraped. For some businesses, depending on industry, this might have been more threatening. Some may have done something about it internally, but most simply let it slide. Around the year 2000 (remember when y2k sounded futuristic and edgy?), the legal concerns became more important. It first came up when eBay filed a preliminary injunction against a company they knew was scraping their website information, because a company as large as eBay had much more at stake than most websites in the 1990s. This action brought up the question: Is scraping legal, and if not, exactly when is it illegal?

The issue came up again in 2001 when a travel agency sued another company for scraping its information. The rival company had been making use of pricing information without consent for the sole purpose of undercutting the competition. This brought direct attention to the importance of determining whether a company has authorized or unauthorized access of information. The next question was: How do websites ensure that no unauthorized users could be scraping information?

To this day, it is very difficult to determine if scraping is legal or not. There are many arguments for both sides. One prime example is travel sites. The costs of a company's various vacation options are most likely available on the site. Therefore, the information a rival company gathers isn't private. The company could have hired an intern to legally search the site and gather the information, but they used scraping as a more efficient way of gathering that information instead. Is that illegal? Web scraping is often a tactic of people who don't want to be identified. With the anonymizing techniques of today, it's tough to pinpoint exactly who did what, which makes it difficult to say definitively whether a scrape was illegal or not. However, it is possible to identify scraping activity, so while companies may not have the ability to catch the scraper, there can discover how the information is being scraped. This means that they can stop it from happening, or at least prevent it from happening in the same way again.

Can you truly prevent web scraping? It is possible to guard your website and set up ways to identify it when it happens, and it's also possible to block some scrapers, especially those less advanced. But stopping scraping entirely is virtually impossible. This isn't to say you shouldn't make an attempt to protect yourself. If you ever find yourself in a courtroom arguing over the legalities of someone scraping your site, the court will want to see that you did something to protect yourself. It's far easier to claim information was stolen when it wasn't made readily available. For example, if someone steals your bike while it's sitting unguarded and unchained on the sidewalk, the thief could claim that they simply found the bike. If your bike is chained in your garage and guarded by a pair of insane Dobermans, though, it makes the "I found it" claim a much tougher sell.

There is software you can use called CAPTCHA. Unfortunately, most scrapers know ways to get around this, and as they do, there will be updates to the software in an attempt to keep pace with the scrapers. The more you update and maintain your protective software, the harder the scraper has to work. By stepping up your game, you ensure that the scraper knows he's crossing into illegal waters, which may in itself keep him from digging into your site.

In the end, there is only one thing of which to be sure. As long as web scraping offers a competitive advantage, companies will do it. And most likely, these scrapers are looking for flaws in service or ways to undercut prices, both of which are considered virtues in a capitalist system. This puts web scraping in a legal gray zone from which it isn't likely to escape.

That doesn't mean we can't identify a clear line between legal and illegal or determine if you're at risk. Bots are almost always used in web scraping. Legitimate bots are identified by the company or organization using them. If bots are kosher, users openly admit they are implementing them. Today, one such company openly doing web scraping is Google. Google bots identify themselves within their HTTP header. Obviously, if they were up to something shady, they wouldn't put their name on it, right? Illegal bots (Terminator theme music in the background) will often have a false company name or impersonate legitimate companies. The next obvious tell is that legitimate bots stick to a site's robot.txt file. This is slightly more advanced computer language, but it basically lists which pages a bot may access and which it may not. An illegal scraper won't abide by these standards. Regardless of what a site has deemed acceptable, the bot will go where it pleases and take what it wants. This would be a clear indicator to the courts that the practice is illegal.

The resources and money required to run web scraper bots is massive. This is because it takes entire servers to process the massive amounts of harvested data. This doesn't mean it's impossible for someone to do it on a strict budget. A scrappy, can-do individual could use a botnet (multiple computers, often spread out over states or countries, that are all infected with the same malware and all controlled from a home base). The owners of the botnet computers don't know that their system is infected or that they are participating in the scraping. This means the perpetrator can scrape from many different websites while the owners of the computers go about their normal web browsing. We'll dive even deeper into all things botnet in chapter seven.

Chapter 6 -- Backdoors

Backdoors are very much what they sound like, but more technical than hidden buttons or deceptive icons that coax you into clicking them. We're talking about a system, method, or software that is hidden to bypass normal authentication and allows an administrator or hacker to enter undocumented (like those hidden passages in Clue). In short, it's a sneaky backdoor someone can create and use to gain access continuously without you knowing it.

Backdoors can be used again and again, one of the main differences between them and other issues we've discussed so far. Backdoors can be used on a number of devices, including routers. They may be used to gain access to software itself or to gain entry to a website. They aren't necessarily used illegally or maliciously. Often, backdoors are created so that an administrator can gain access and make updates or troubleshoot. Sometimes, we find them used in a gray area such as when intelligence agencies employ them to gather information. That dives into the question of the invasion of privacy, but the bottom line is that you use backdoors when you want continual access without anyone knowing.

Most backdoors are created intentionally by legitimate users for legitimate purposes rather than by hackers. They may be created with unchangeable credentials (username and password), they may be built with the capacity to add and change credentials whenever necessary, or they may be designed without any credentials needed at all. Most often, the backdoor exists without the owner knowing it. For example, large software companies often have backdoors installed so they can fix issues without you ever knowing there was a problem in the first place, thus maintaining your faith in their product. However, even if a backdoor is created with the purest of intentions, its existence pokes a hole in the security. A backdoor is a point of entry that any hacker worth his bitcoin will be sure to exploit.

If a hacker wants to create a backdoor, she will most likely do it by installing malware such as a Remote Access Trojan (RAT), which then allows her to install even more software or pull important data.

In case you have the feeling you've read about these methods before, that may be because backdoors gained notoriety when Edward Snowden leaked the NSA documents to the media in 2013. He revealed that for years spy agencies had worked with Britain's GCHQ to pressure companies to install backdoors into their own products. Primarily, this was about the agencies gaining access to encryption and security software so that they could get in and gather data. This is an example of the use of backdoors on a grand scale.

But let's bring things a little closer to home. Why should you concern yourself with backdoors? For one, they allow hackers to create, delete, rename, copy, or edit any file. They can change executive commands. They can change system settings. They can even run, control, and terminate applications. This means that they can also add software and viruses. On a very basic level, they can start, restart, or shutdown your computer whenever they want. They can steal personal information, including your browsing history, passwords, and so forth. This is an excellent way for someone to steal your entire digital identity. Without your knowledge, they can send and copy your entire system to a server or "machine gun" email your entire contact list, including individuals with whom you've never corresponded. From your point of view, you may only notice a slowdown in your Internet service because of this activity, or you may suddenly find your entire system has been wiped. We mentioned in an earlier chapter that when hackers want to get into web scraping, they sometimes use other people's computers to do their dirty work. Installing a backdoor is one of the most common ways for them to pull this off. Really, once the backdoor is there, they can use your system for anything they want (and that "anything" typically isn't the betterment of mankind).

At this point, you're probably getting a little freaked out, and rightfully so. But before you take a sledgehammer to your family PC and feed the pieces into your garbage disposal, let's look at how you can protect yourself and, if need be, eliminate any existing backdoors in your system.

A backdoor can get into your system through everyday activity. Web browsing, email, or bundling other software you might download from the Internet are the most common ways. It's crucial that you have anti-virus software and scan things like emails before opening, especially on PCs. A lot of email services have some of this built in, but it's imperative that you pay attention to the warnings when they pop up. We've all gotten annoyed when we see a pop-up for an email address we trust. However, it may not actually be your friend emailing you; their email may have been hijacked with a virus embedded into it (the figurative wolf in sheep's clothing). They may unwittingly be helping a hacker send out the virus or malware. When you download new software from the Internet, you should scan it, or at the very least make sure it comes from a trusted website known for its high security.

Besides downloading software, something as simple as a screensaver can actually be the work of hackers disguising their true intent. A good example is WATERFALLS.scr. This was a waterfall screensaver that claimed to be nothing more, but it turned out to be associated with malware and would release a Trojan that unloaded programs, even giving its creator access to your system. Backdoors don't need large or complicated files to hide. This means you should be careful of everything you download. The lesson here: Don't go chasing waterfalls.

Downloading isn't the only way to get a backdoor on your system. You may accidentally transfer malware via a hard drive or USB flash drive. Technically, any portable media can have malware on it (incriminating photos from the office party not included). Sometimes it just comes down to you being forced to reformat the drive to avoid transferring it to other devices. This doesn't sound that bad, but depending on the drive, you may be losing valuable data or files. Often, malware is designed in such a way that simply trying to back up a few files from the drive results in unknowingly transferring the malware. Trying to transfer those beloved Disney photos from one device to another will mean duplicating the backdoor if one of the files is corrupted.

A virus is going to duplicate itself over and over, but a Trojan only needs to get on your system once to create an effective back door. On the surface, it can seem safe or even pointless, but it's actually opening up your entire system to attack. Combined with the fact that a backdoor grants access over and over, this makes it easy to see why the things are such a concern and can be difficult to locate manually.

If it's so easy to get one and so hard to find it once it's there, how do you eliminate a backdoor after you've been had? Luckily, there are plenty of automatic removal options. Many programs are available to find and root out backdoors. However, this isn't something you should just go online to search, download, and assume will be done while you scoot off to the loo. Running the software could cause issues with pre-existing software or valuable files. Make sure to update these programs before launching the tool, as it will minimize the risk of failures and other issues.

More and more companies are popping up every day to offer security and protection. Because there are so many options out there, you have to be very careful before picking one. Many of these options are designed to protect against more than one type of malware, ransomware and virus. Don't just download the first you find without determining if it will meet all your needs. The most well-known vendors, such as McAfee, Symantec, AVG Anti-Virus, Malwarebytes, etc. cover viruses, spyware, adware, and other threats, but they're *reactive* solutions that can only inoculate what they know about. (This is not an endorsement of any of these products, by the way. Unfortunately for me, I am receiving zero compensation from these companies.)

For instance, an anti-spyware such as Malwarebytes not only detects spyware, but it also removes Trojans, rootkits, and whatever other threats it finds in its inoculation code database. I can't stress enough how important it is that you protect yourself against viruses, malware, spyware, and Trojans and have something installed to help you remove threats once found.

Attacks come in many forms, and so do prevention options. Be prepared and realistic about the risks associated with these potential attacks and ensure you're doing whatever it takes to protect yourself.

However, these reactive solutions are only one very small piece of the puzzle. This particular security layer that alone only accounts for less than 5% of overall security effectiveness.

If you'd like a *proactive* solution, there is a new, recently declassified, internationally patented cybersecurity solution that has a 10-year track record in stopping all zero day malware and ransomware. Call us toll free at 1-877-468-2721 to learn more.

According to CBS News: https://www.cbsnews.com/news/kasperksy-lab-software-suspected-ties-russian-intelligence-rob-joyce/ Kaspersky Lab Software, a Moscow-based cybersecurity company has suspected ties to Russian intelligence. This means that the software could be spying on your systems and sending data back to the Kremlin without your knowledge.

SECTION THREE – MALWARE

It's time to dive deeper into malware. We will be discussing some new terms as well as really cracking into terms we've already discussed. We'll chat about how different aspects of cyber security problems can come together to make your life harder than it needs to be. Malware lives in a family of resources at the fingertips of malicious hackers trying to find ways to make money off your system or device. Because of the sheer number of threats and the evolving nature of attacks, there are no guarantees that you can avoid infection entirely. But the idea behind cyber security is to do everything you can to protect yourself from as many threats as possible, thereby lowering your risk of getting creamed.

First, we will discuss botnets, which we have already covered briefly. In that chapter, we will expand your knowledge of how botnets work and why they are implemented. We will then discuss data corruption. The more you know about the various ways data corruption can occur, the easier it will be to determine when malware is at fault. Finally, you'll need to grab your metaphorical shovel, because we will dig into the dirty topic of ransomware. Quickly becoming a household word, ransomware (which is nowhere near as convenient as Tupperware) comes in different forms and presents varying issues. When we're done, you'll no doubt feel fortunate that you've never gotten first-hand experience with it (and if you have, you'll relive the nightmare, for which I sincerely apologize). And you will surely understand the importance of protecting yourself against it. It could cost you your prized iTunes gift card, but let's wait to get into that in Chapter 9.

I should probably warn you, though. As you read the information in this section, things can start to seem hopeless. Plug in a night light if you need to, but don't let that feeling overwhelm you and drive you down the path to a "straight from the carton" Ben and Jerry's binge. We will highlight the options available to you, and in the final section, we will explore the steps you can take to protect yourself. This section is all about educating yourself on what you are defending your systems against. Understanding the criminals and their weapons will make you less likely to be victimized.

Chapter 7 - Botnet

As we discussed in chapter 5, a botnet is a network of multiple computers used by one hacker. All the systems are infected with the same malware and are often controlled by the same home base (or at least sending data back to the home base). Picture a deranged puppeteer with thousands of strings on his devious little fingers. Now change the puppets to computers and the strings to wires, and you've got the idea. The owners of the computers have no idea it's happening. They merrily keep working at their computers, oblivious to the fact that they're helping collect data for hackers.

"Botnet" is a combination of the word robot and the word network. There is always a level of remote work involved in the use of botnets. If you recall in the previous chapter, we mentioned that hackers use botnets to save money on resources by tapping into equipment owned by others (you, for example). They may not have the means to buy up multiple systems to run the spam, or they may just be unwilling to put their own resources out there. They outsource the work to multiple systems, not only to avoid the high cost of setting up such an operation, but also to avoid detection.

In addition to the benefit of additional computing power from the large network of infected systems, botnets are desirable tools for cybercriminals because they offer a spread across multiple geographic locations. This spreads the hack across multiple ISP addresses as well as states and countries, and it diversifies the "accomplices" who actually own the systems within the botnet.

This does not mean that botnets are strictly a web of computers in the home desktop sense. They can make full use of PCs, servers, mobile devices, and anything else that might run through the Internet and has the ability to download malware. (Your old-school VHS player is safe.) And don't make the mistake of imagining that the mess stops at just 15 or 20 devices employed by the hacker. Any given botnet around the world could be as extensive as 20,000 machines. Hardcore botnet operators would even see this large of a pool of employed devices as amateur hour. There are accounts of advanced botnets that stretch into the millions.

For the botnet operator, there are multiple ways to make money off of such a network of unknown "employees." For one, imagine the hacker or operator of the botnet like a landlord. They rent out the service of their botnet, meaning other cyber criminals or hackers can pay to make use of this massive asset. The more systems that have been infected by the malware, the prettier the penny the botnet lord can demand for its use. They might sell or rent the network, but there are many legal considerations for the hacker. In the end, the use is normally the same. Whoever ends up controlling the botnet will most likely use it for a large spamming campaign.

Part of why hackers want to sprawl across so many different locations, computers, or uses has to do with the nature of trying to find people to rent out their botnet. The creator of the botnet wants to expand his portfolio. The malware itself may seek different things so that they are pointed in several non-related goals. There are Bedep botnets, which only host malware as a download source for an exploit kit. Another type would be Kovter botnets, primarily used to host ransomware, which we will discuss more in depth in an upcoming chapter.

A Bedep botnet is a Trojan horse that opens the backdoor that's already in place within the system. It also downloads additional files. There has been a lot of press around Bedeps recently. Google even began targeting Bedeps specifically. The problem caught their attention when more than 500,000 machines, desktops, tablets, and smartphones were reported infected by Bedep, Beetal, or Changthangi. (Everyone loves an epidemic, right?) The entire purpose is to gain remote access of the computer. In order to accomplish this, the malware makes certain changes on the system. It will most likely focus changes on registry and firewall settings. It's designed to steal sensitive data from the PC and then store it on a section of a hard drive configured to send everything along to the hacker. The malicious code is embedded on a file attached to a spam email message. Opening the spam runs the malware without you realizing it. The ugly little thing can also get ahold of you from a link in the comments area of a blog site, social networking site, or cracked program.

Kovter is another type of Trojan horse, and its primary purpose is running click-fraud operations on the systems it infects. In 2015, Kovter added new cloaking tricks to avoid detection. This makes it popular with cybercriminals who aim to deliver other types of malware such as ransomware or who want to acquire more systems for botnets. By definition, a Trojan is malware without the ability to spread all by itself. You must run the programs or visit a webpage to get the ball rolling. Kovter is designed to be file-less after infection, which means there are fewer breadcrumbs to follow. Sometimes its sole purpose is loading more malware into the system.

In either case, the symptoms of infection can vary, as can the file names under which your software might find it. Symptoms include your task manager showing numerous occurrences of mshta.exe or powershell.exe processes running. Pages may be blocked or unreachable when you browse the Internet. The system might slow down or begin running like a sedated slug, and programs take longer to start up. Unusual disk activity is a major clue. You may get alerts or notifications that PowerShell has "stopped working." You will normally see it coming up under names like Win32:Kovter-C, Trojan.Kotver!gen1, Trojan.Ransomlock.AK, Trojan/Kovter.c, and so forth. (If something with "Trojan" in the name was to pop up and that wouldn't be a waving red flag for you, please go back to chapter 1 for another run through.)

Protecting your computer from infection begins with security software, of course. Anti-malware is a common product push in your email for a reason. This is where the malware gets not only complex but also quite clever. They are often designed to automatically scan the system they've infiltrated for common vulnerabilities that haven't been fixed or updated. It's a numbers game as they try to get into as many systems as possible in as many ways as they can to control them in the background without attracting notice. The bad guys look for things like ineffective or outdated security products, so the benefits of these protections are only as good as your diligence in keeping them updated. When you do purchase anti-virus software and malware protection, be certain you download it directly from the official product site. Third-party websites can be a trap for sneaking nasty malware into your system through the very file you're downloading for protection.

In addition to the anti-virus and other anti-malware protections, a powerful way to guard yourself from attack is with Zero Day Plus (ZDP). This little chestnut stands between malicious malware and your computer by preventing the bad executable program(s) from writing to your hard drive. If the malware can't drop its payload, then it can't run and do its damage if it can't access your computer's processing power in the first place.

Mac computers are thought to be more secure, however, there is still malware and ransomware that targets Mac users. If you're on a PC using Windows, Microsoft's Malicious Software Removal Tool (MSRT) can be a great step in removing botnet-related malware. Using the Windows automatic update, you can have this tool run once per month automatically. This is a smart way to stay protected when your busy schedule gets in the way, or you pick up a "harmless" addiction to free app games that might be running malware in the background. (Knocking the funny little animal off his log might do more than land you on a PETA watch list.)

Some Internet providers offer some protection, and you may have seen notices popping up when some kind of botnet traffic has been detected. If one of these comes up from your ISP, use the Malicious

Software Removal Tool or some similar protocol. If it comes up too often (or never seems to go away), get a computer professional to check your system.

Chapter 8 - Data corruption

Most computer owners and cell phone owners are familiar with data corruption. There are more than enough ways for it to happen, and this curse can strike any kind of hard drive or file. It usually develops subtly. You may notice it when you're in the middle of a big work project, desperate to make a good impression on a client, only to discover that the files you pulled an all-nighter to perfect are suddenly no longer accessible.

Data corruption is deterioration or damage caused by hardware, software, or human error. The possible causes are as numerous as bugs in a swamp, but there are some basic steps you can take to prevent data corruption. Keep a daily eye out for symptoms. You don't have to start every day by scanning your system, as that could realistically be a time management concern. But do take the time to dig deeper when you come across any kind of hiccup in your normal workflow. When something wonky goes down, check your disks and files for any kind of error to lower the chances of real damage. Like that receding hairline or your eye-twitching intolerance for Dora the

Explorer's voice, data corruption is something that grows with time, so your goal is to stop it before it becomes a serious problem and costs you your sanity. It's just like keeping track of your own physical health by getting a check-up when you aren't sick. (You do, in fact, do that... right? Riiiiiight?)

Listed below are some of the "hiccups" that serve as a warning that you need to check whether corruption has begun or taken hold of your computer. (Note that holding your breath will not solve these types of problems.) Organization is extremely important in your folder and subfolder workflow. This makes it easier to notice if files or folders are suddenly relocated or missing. Open your files regularly just to make sure they haven't become infected. Receiving an open file error such as "invalid file format" can be a sign that corruption has started. Do files suddenly get renamed with gibberish or random characters? If you start seeing that file permissions and attributes are suddenly modified, that could be another red flag. If your system keeps crashing and lagging for no apparent reason, you most definitely need to take action. Your disk slowing down all together is also a key indicator, and you should sit up and pay attention if disk activities appear to be super busy even when you are procrastinating and not doing anything but bingeing on the latest episodes of *Better Call Saul*.

One of the most common causes of data corruption is a bad program exit. Bad exits occur when you switch off or restart a computer without using the proper shutdown procedure. Much like choosing to break up with someone via text rather than in person, this is a convenient shortcut that can come back later to bite you right in the face. This simple act of switching off in a hurry could be a quick ticket to data corruption city. An unintentional power failure that catches you and your electronics by surprise can have the same effect. There are battery backup power strips you can purchase to avoid this sadistic twist of fate, but you can't always do anything to avoid these situations. Software can lock up and system errors can freeze your machine, giving you no option but to restart your computer. When a file is only halfway written or a process is halted, the file creation becomes incomplete and the corruption occurs. To avoid your software crashing or freezing, maintain a safe Internet connection and always run updates directly supplied by the software developer.

The next data corruption culprit is physical defects. This is when hardware functionality leads to the corruption of data being processed or stored. This is most commonly from regular wear and tear and the deterioration of a component over time. Things like "disk head crash" and "bad sector" are known for causing permanent damage. Fortunately, new technology now comes with diagnostic tests that will report and warn you before the failure happens.

The third source of data corruption is poorly written software. Major companies like Adobe have built customer loyalty because they aren't known for having issues like this. A more common example of developers creating poorly written software shows up with all those new programs you see advertised. They pop up claiming that if you download now, they can do many things your old software can't, and they're cheaper while they do it! These new companies may be bringing new innovations to the table, but because they are new and unknown, you must ask yourself: How tested is this software? How well has it been checked for bugs? A very large percentage of reported data corruption comes from shoddy software. Much of the freeware and shareware available online is poorly written in ways that can result in system instability and other thorny issues. A big complaint from users is when programs start making changes to your system settings without your consent or that keep you from later removing the software completely. They may leave loads of junk that occupy redundant storage areas in your hard disk and system registry. Keep this in mind when you are tempted to install something (like the knock-off version of the highly addictive Candy Crush or the major time-suck Words with Friends), and always do your due diligence before downloading. Check reviews and forums about it.

That "little nothing" software you want to try could contain utilities that secretly house spyware.

Malware is easily the second most common cause of data corruption. When you read about malware, it's usually in reference to a software program created to inflict damage to a system. (It's sort of like your crazy ex friending you on Facebook and then posting compromising photos of you). It may not be the primary or only function of the software. Many viruses replicate and overwrite areas of raw disk with junk that ends up just overloading and eating up space. The truly devious ones designed by super-villain masterminds of the everyday execute undesirable operations such as deleting files, modifying data, and stimulating typos to destroy document files and operating system files. You may notice that your computer suddenly has excessive activity.

Viruses also slow down your computer or device by drawing extra processor cycles when they execute their own code. Very advanced viruses, such as a boot sector virus, embed themselves in the system errors and corrupt the partition sector. This cripples your computer when you turn it on. Eliminating malware is thus crucial for computer users who do, in fact, want to use their computers. Your level of risk depends on your choice of applications. If you're constantly downloading programs from the Internet, you must be more careful than those who don't. (You know who you are, Battlefield fans.) It should go without saying that poorly written software can come with not only glitches in its making, but malware as well.

After you've selected the antivirus software to protect your system, the next thing on your to do list should be identifying and removing any little uglies that have already made themselves at home within your system. After removing them, maximize your protection by selecting "real-time" mode rather than "on-access" mode. You do this within the software settings, and it isn't too complicated for the average Joe. The "real-time" background mode tells your antivirus software to scan every file that enters the memory or microprocessor. The "on-access" mode only performs a scan when you manually tell it to initiate the program and begin a scan. Some of the best advice when it comes to cyber security is to avoid human error by making sure the protection you have operates automatically, or at the very least has reminders and notifications in place so that it'll actually be used.

This includes keeping on top of updates whenever possible. It's imperative to have your settings such that the computer will run the updates for your antivirus software on its own or regularly remind you to initiate them. Always stay on top of updates and operating system patches so you can protect against vulnerabilities within the operating system or software. Hackers love updates, because they announce the existing vulnerabilities to the world (including the hacker herself, who may not have been aware of the flaw before the update shed light on it), and then software users have this nasty little habit of ignoring update patches that fix the exposed weakness. In a way, failing to take advantage of updates is like having someone point out to you in public that your fly is open and then just standing there like a doofus, doing nothing about it while the people around you stare.

All the constant updates and scans can seem like a hassle, but anyone who has dealt with data corruption can tell you that the updates are well worth the time. Often, users complain that they don't understand why they can't just use their system without issues. They look to the maker of their laptop to place blame. Keep in mind that Dell makes computers the way Chevy makes cars. Chevy isn't at fault because car thieves exist. They do what they can to create better security systems, but the thief is also learning new ways to get around those security systems. The same goes for computers and devices. Computer companies do what they can to avoid making it too easy for things like malware to cause data corruption. Chances are, you'll have to deal with data corruption on some level, but if you're consistent in the suggestions we have gone through, you can minimize the damage and frequency of occurrence.

You should always look at current ratings and protection offers when buying a new system. This year's product may be better than last year's... or it could be worse. Don't assume that because you got a certain type of computer or device five years ago that the company is just as up-to-date with their protection today as they were when you bought your machine. Take the time to do research on forums and review sites. Look at the antivirus software you use with the same scrutiny. The hackers and their malware want you to get comfortable and skip the update or change these securities. Unfortunately, malware is hidden within many different products and systems for delivery into your computer, making it a never-ending issue for users, just as crime is for police enforcement. The end result of data corruption is a large price to pay for not doing your part to keep your system safe.

Your best defense against data corruption is prevention. Maintaining diligent attempts to prevent such occurrences can seem costly and/or time-consuming up front, but what price would you put on your data? Family photos, contact lists, and embarrassing videos used to blackmail your children may be just the tip of the iceberg. What about employee records? What about invoicing information? What about client presentations? Think of the most valuable thing on your system, and then ask yourself whether prevention seems too big of an investment to keep it safe.

Chapter 9 - Ransomware

Ransomware has come up frequently in previous sections. It sounds like something made up for an action thriller, but the movies tend to romanticize what can feel very much like a cyber criminal holding you up at the ATM. In reality, it's an infection that will lock you out of your hard drive or entire system until you pay a literal ransom to get it removed. The average cost is around $300, but that is only the typical sum extortionists demand for the safe return of what was rightfully yours. Since you're a small business, you have more at stake than would a private individual; you're more likely to be desperate to have your computer and data restored immediately. Supply and demand, sweetheart. You're in business, so you know what demand does to prices, right? Right. You end up cornered into paying an absurd amount of money for the "service" of having the perpetrator restore access to your encrypted files or locked computers. It's horrifyingly easy to get infected with ransomware, and we have already mentioned ways it can happen. Although it's a cliché that people get hit like this because they can't resist a glimpse of Jenna Jameson's latest porn venture or because they naively open every little spam window that pops up, the truth is that it can happen to anyone. Even if you don't do anything too lascivious or stupid, you're still at risk.

Ransomware isn't just something that hits corporate servers and master controls. Personal laptops, tablets, and even smart phones are juicy targets. They either lock you out or encrypt your files, thus holding them ransom.

There are basically two types of ransomware. One is called a crypto. This type will encrypt files and refuse you access. To decrypt them, you must have the key that was used when encryption occurred. The second type is called a blocker. They block a computer or electronic device from being useful. You have a much better chance of getting rid of a block on access than decrypting without purchasing the key, so these two types of ransomware are not created equal.

As I mentioned a minute ago, the average cost of getting access restored is around $300, but there's a big difference between one end of the spectrum and the other. Some ransomware programs may charge just $30, which is still annoying and traumatizing, albeit on a smaller scale. Others may ask for tens of thousands of dollars, at which point you'll long for the simple sweetness of annoyance. Industry leaders and massive corporations tend to get hit with record-breaking ransoms. They are often infected through what is called *spear phishing*. Spear phishing is when fake emails are sent out to specific organizations, groups, or individuals in an attempt to trick the receiver into giving away confidential information. It can include various levels of impersonation, incitement, and access-control bypass techniques like email filters and antivirus. Like the general concept of phishing, spear phishing is often just a more targeted attempt to get the receiver to open an attachment or click on an embedded link. Although this is not a commonly employed tactic used for ransomware, it can certainly be a means to gain access.

Let's say that you do get hit with ransomware. The first question you might ask is whether you can get your file decrypted without paying, and if so, how? Frankly, as we mentioned before, decryption without the key is neither easy nor common. Ransomware programs usually use very advanced and resilient crypto algorithms. In simple terms, it could take years to gain access, and by then, any business-related information is bound to be irrelevant. You may as well just chuck your computer in the trash and start from scratch. But what about catching the crook, you ask? There have been cases where the criminals behind these types of attacks make mistakes. On account of these mistakes, law enforcement can sometimes catch these criminals. Seizing the actual servers used in the attack can mean that police are able to retrieve the keys themselves. They can then release the key, and you get to be one of the lucky few that get their files back without paying. However, because this scenario is quite rare, many people and companies choose to pay the fee and be done with the nightmare. But let's be real. This in no way guarantees that you will see a safe and reliable return of access to your device because, after all, you are dealing with a criminal. They don't exactly care about providing good customer service. Sometimes they take your ransom and laugh all the way to the bank, knowing that you paid them for nothing. Research shows that 20% of ransomware victims who pay the fee don't ever get their files back. The solution? It's simple: Don't get ransomware in the first place.

When it appears that you're on your own and the government doesn't seem to be hot on the case, the only choice you're left with is the gamble of paying in the hopes that the ransomware will be removed. But how do you pay? I hate to tell you this, but there's no glamor in it. Maybe it would be exciting if you got a phone call, a distorted voice on the other end telling you a location and time for dropping a bag full of unmarked bills. At least then you'd have a story to tell at parties on the other side of the experience. Unfortunately, the reality is something a little more grounded in the world of the Internet. Bitcoins or other cryptocurrency is normally the preferred method of payment, as it's a form of currency that cannot be forged. Although the transaction history may be available to the public, the wallet owner cannot be easily identified or tracked, which is why it is the choice of payment by cyber criminals everywhere. Anything they can do to lower their chances of being caught, they're going to do it. Some types of ransomware will have an anonymous online wallet or even mobile payment methods. One of the most surprising common forms of payment is an iTunes gift card. Perhaps the criminals just use them as stocking stuffers for loved ones around the holidays. More likely, though, it's their wide acceptability and reliability that makes them so preferred.

It's extremely common for ransomware to come to you in email. It may pose as a useful attachment or something important, like an urgent financial document. There may be offers for things like free downloads, free upgrades, or free apps. The attachment is the poisoned apple. Once you open it, you become like Snow White and have swallowed the poison. You must get the antidote, a solution that is very unlikely to be a kiss from a handsome prince. Email isn't the only way you can get infected. Even just surfing the Internet can expose you to ransomware. A hacker or his software can gain control of your system through OS, browsers, and app vulnerabilities. As mentioned before, all the updates you see are often the very patches they hope you won't download. That means even cautious users can get infected. Sites that hold your attention can get you. If the site is a news outlet of some kind, and the stories are long enough that any reader may be there for a prolonged time, it's a great place to infect. The website will most likely be completely unaware that this is taking place. They aren't trying to hack their visitors. In fact, in some situations, the entire site may be compromised and under the control of the ransomware creator.

Some ransomware has been known to self-propagate through local networks. If a Trojan of that kind infects one machine or device in your personal or business network, it will eventually make its way into others. The infection will spread until it is dealt with properly. However, this is rare, as self-propagation is more complex and requires a more sophisticated ransomware. More common infection scenarios involve things like downloading a torrent or installing a new plugin. Your current antivirus hasn't been updated, it fails to catch the embedded ransomware, and boom! You're infected.

Suspicious files tend to be executable files (EXE or SCR) with visual basic scripts or JavaScript. They also tend to be concealed in ZIP or RAR folders. This is an excellent delivery system because you can't see what's inside until you open it. Microsoft Office files such as DOC, DOCX, XLS, and PPT are dangerous. A clue is that they often prompt you to enable macros in a Word document. This should raise red flags. Shortcut files with the extension LNK are also common hiding places. Because they can be assigned any icon, it's easy for them to set you up to click before you've had a chance to think about it. In fact, if you're in Windows, you should make sure that your preferences and settings are such that extensions are always visible. This will help you spot suspicious activity. For instance, the name of a file may be ImportantInfo.doc. (It is unlikely to be labeled Ransomwares-R-Us.doc, sadly.) It looks as if you're seeing the extension, but once you change your setting to show extensions, you might discover that it now shows as Important Info.doc.exe. The EXE is the real extension, and the true nature of the file is a malware installer.

To all those Apple enthusiasts out there, I have some disheartening news. Macs aren't entirely safe from ransomware. For example, a massive ransomware hit Mac users who visited a transmission torrent client. Many security software providers and forums believe that Apple systems will be targeted more and more in the future. Since Apple products are often more expensive than PCs, it's likely that hackers will demand higher ransoms to grant release from Mac-based ransomware. Even more atypical, but still formally documented, are ransomware attacks on Linux users. The longer a specific product, operating system, or software exists, the more likely it is that someone out there is working on malware to attack it. Remember, this isn't just computers we're talking about. Even Android cellphones have cryptos and blockers available, and you would be wise to consider them. Antivirus for smartphones is going to be more and more of a concern, especially with people linking bank accounts and other financial information to their smartphones through apps.

Currently, there don't seem to be any iPhone or iPod ransomware programs, but that just means no one has publicly discussed being hit by one, and no one has been caught making one. Part of this is because Apple's app store is extremely locked down. It's far more difficult to get an app approved for sale within their store, so this creates a high level of protection. The more products and devices become "smart," the more likely we are to see malware designed for them. This means products like Apple TVs could be threatened by ransomware attacks in the near future.

As these new forms come out and ransomware becomes more of a public spectacle, we can track them more easily. Petya is different because, instead of encrypting files one by one, it denies access to the full system by attacking low-level structures on the disk. CryptXXX has been known to be very powerful and has come back to hit some victims more than once. TeslaCrypt is another fun one. Frankly, the more public these types of ransomware become, the harder it is for hackers to hide. The more consumers demand protection, the more advanced security software will become.

If you are infected, you don't have to concern yourself with trying to figure it out on your own. It will announce itself very clearly (just like your nosy mother-in-law). A window of some kind will come up and tell you that you are blocked. It won't let your computer load operating systems or allow you to do any basic functions. There are many online options you can try in the hopes of removing the blocker and getting Windows to boot. This does not always mean you gain full access, however. If you get hit with a crypto, things will be much harder. We discussed this earlier, but your first option is to get rid of the malware by running an antivirus scan. If you have backup copies of your files, consider yourself as lucky as the latest Powerball winner (but hopefully less likely to declare bankruptcy within a few years); just restore your files and you're good to go.

If you don't have backups, you can attempt decrypting options in special utilities called decryptors. Even if you are quick to get a decryptor, you must realize that the hacker making malware knows that these are coming out rapidly. They will go out of their way to make sure they have done what they can to stay resilient against the newest decryptors, so in the end, there are simply no guarantees.

SECTION FOUR – DEFENDING DATA AND DEVICES

Now we're going to cover the steps you can and should take in order to protect your organization from the multitude of problems and pitfalls awaiting you out there. One of the first things we need to do is to understand these threats and how they work. Understanding thy enemy is crucial in beating them. (Some general said that at some point; I'm sure of it.) In any case, knowledge is power, and the better understanding you have of these threats, the more potent your defense can be. Obviously.

Also, in the event that you are breached, a thorough working knowledge of these threats will most certainly help mitigate the damage and make the salvage process a lot easier.

Regardless of what you learn from this material, it is paramount that you understand this is a continuing process. You have to stay on top of this mess. When you consider the speed and rapidity of technological evolution, just imagine the underbelly of the digital realm with legions of evil-doing techno geeks with nothing else to do all day but invent new and interesting ways to toy with your organization. This requires constant vigilance, and that is perhaps the most important lesson.

Now it's all well and good that you've taken the first step in actually *reading* about cyber-security. Now you also have to acknowledge that this can be and will likely become a very complicated procedure. There are the more common steps anyone can take to protect themselves, which amounts to anti-malware downloads, etc., but it's likely not going to be enough in the case of even smaller enterprises. This is especially true if you're involved in safeguarding personal and sensitive information of clients or patients. In short, you'd likely benefit from a professional consultation to implement more comprehensive coverage for you company.

Just like any other segment of the population, there are those that simply will not or cannot play by the rules, and the virtual community is no different. In fact, it can be daunting to even consider how many miscreants are out there, quietly and anonymously working to overcome the latest in cyber protection in order to steal, extort, or hold ransom your information and resources. Some rich dude once speculated that one of the surest ways to building wealth is to let your money work for you. Hackers employ this philosophy as they go about their business, laying traps or phishing in order to snag unsuspecting innocents who double click without thinking; meanwhile they're working on some next-level nightmare in order to remain a step ahead of the proverbial slowest buffalo.

Given how complicated the subject of cyber-security is, we're gonna do our best to keep the material presented as simple and as easy to follow as we can for the sake of understanding and future reference. These next couple-few chapters will focus on the steps you can take to protect yourself, the need to stay ahead of the game, and what to consider when choosing your IT security guru.

Chapter 10 -- Steps Anyone Can Take to Defend Themselves

The first thing we'll cover are the basics that anyone can do to defend against cyber breaches. Some of them we've already covered, but hey -- it doesn't hurt to be refreshed.

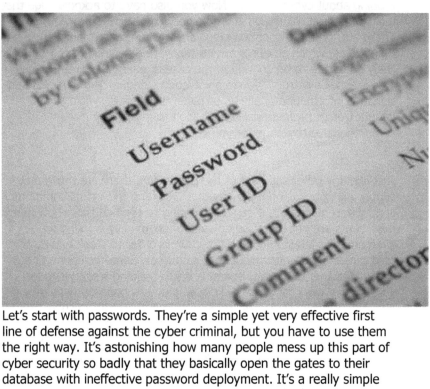

Let's start with passwords. They're a simple yet very effective first line of defense against the cyber criminal, but you have to use them the right way. It's astonishing how many people mess up this part of cyber security so badly that they basically open the gates to their database with ineffective password deployment. It's a really simple concept, and everyone knows this, but don't use the same passwords over and over. Also, it's not really that clever to merely attach numbers to the end of your password and think that's gonna do the trick. Do yourself and your clients a huge favor by using passwords that aren't obvious, and change them up often enough to keep hackers guessing. While some websites insist you use your email as an online ID, you can create email accounts strictly for these purposes; this will mitigate risk and keep your real email, business or personal, out of the line of fire.

And while it may seem obvious, there are some people out there (quite possibly you, Dear Reader) that need to be warned about storing passwords digitally, be it in the cloud or in the overall digital-sphere where anyone can root around and eventually find it. This simply isn't acceptable practice when safeguarding and protecting data. An even worse idea is to email your list of passwords to yourself, especially if the subject line actually says PASSWORDS. Please. I beg you. Don't do that.

In choosing a password, be creative, yet keep it easy enough to remember without the need to write it down. Some people prefer to utilize some cockamamie combination of letters and symbols and numbers that require either a photographic memory or for the password to be written down somewhere. The illusion of safety from such a complex series of characters discourages folks from changing their passwords. Instead, try using a phrase or a short sentence (which easily covers the 8-character minimum you typically find) that makes you laugh and is therefore easy to remember. Just keep in mind that it shouldn't be something that has to do with a passion or something easy for smarter hackers to exploit and ultimately crack your password. For example, ILoveSkittlesMoreThanYou could be a good password for someone who doesn't really care about that particular candy. However, if you're one of those special folks that takes selfies with Skittles in front of national monuments and attractions... then it's not a good idea to use that phrase.

Another thing you need to worry about is physically securing your computer. Even with all the cyber threats and ugliness going on in the digital realm, there still exists the old-fashioned threat of your physical items being stolen by some jerk. Should someone decide to walk away with your computer, there are simple fixes at least to protect data, including signature technologies. This way, if your device disappears or is left unattended, it would at the very least be difficult for anyone to actually get into it. Naturally, a password alongside a thumbprint lock goes a long way in preventing unwanted access, be it from a criminal or the lovely people that you know (such as employees or your creep of an uncle).

As ludicrous as it sounds, and we certainly don't mean to nag, but stop leaving your personal information lying about the work area. A credit card isn't just a means for some criminal to buy a jet ski with your plastic; it's a gateway into the rest of your life as well, including other accounts where you've got more sensitive information available for exploitation. So please, for the love of everything holy, keep your credit cards and other bits of information safely tucked away somewhere, especially when you're not around.

The next thing on the DIY list of protection is to activate your firewall. Although the guy who sold you the computer agreed to throw in the firewall when he talked you into buying this thing in the first place, that does not mean the stuff is actually doing its job straight out of the box. So do make sure it's been activated so that there's something in place to monitor all cyber traffic on this device and ultimately your network. Hopefully, you've also installed the appropriate antivirus software as we've discussed earlier.

The importance of antivirus gear can't be overstated. As we've already covered, regularly updating or purchasing the latest in defense is essential to your security. Astonishingly, research has shown that roughly ten percent of Windows 8 users were running outdated or expired antivirus on their systems, making them vulnerable without even knowing it. Also be sure to use software that can run automatic updates for you, especially if you should be one of those people that are bewildered when it comes to operating computers. There are plenty of safe options out there to make this process easy and so user-friendly that you won't have to think about it.

As we've discussed, but not in particular detail, avoid employing 'cracked' software programs. While it's tempting to go about this whole process as inexpensively as possible, these seemingly cheaper options can lead to a host of other issues, namely the cruel irony that your installed cyber security is how a breach was achieved in the first place. Hackers and criminals will embed some of these programs with their own malware, and this happens more often than people realize. The lesson here is that although you enjoy minimal savings upfront, the overall cost to your organization can be devastating if you're not careful.

When you do get around to installing your software, avoid the mistake of just going along with the manufacturer's recommendations. Take the time to do a custom installation so your device isn't weighed down with needless features, such as those annoying toolbars and other items that mostly serve to bog down the system's operations and eat up memory space. If you're not already familiar with it, get to know your control panel. This is the doorway to safe, effective, and agile use of your antivirus software.

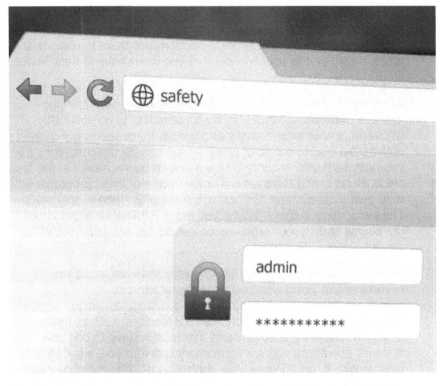

As stated earlier, you shouldn't have your passwords on a document and stored on any device (though I know a remarkable amount of folks will just ignore my advice on that). But in addition to passwords, there are plenty of files and sensitive data that you need to keep protected from the outside. These days, file sharing is nearly a must when it comes to doing business, which brings us to Google Drive, Dropbox, and so on. It's imperative to encrypt these shared files so they're not compromised or providing a hole for criminals and hackers to gain access to your organization's network. While it does take longer and is admittedly a huge pain in the hind quarters, it's still worth the extra effort considering what sort of nonsense awaits you if the worst were to transpire. Think of the time, money, and mental health you could lose all because you were too annoyed or in too much of hurry to take some simple precautions. There's nothing wrong with tedium, especially when compared to consequences.

Let's assume for a moment that you were actually breached. There are ways to mitigate the damage and possibly recoup some losses. For starters, have a plan in place should this happen. After you've contacted the authorities, they're going to want a lot information in order to A) verify that you've been hacked, B) find those responsible, and C) hopefully restore you. If you haven't done so already, find an IT security professional that can handle this for you. They know the language and will understand the details of how everything went down.

Of course... having a cyber security expert in your corner could prevent this nightmare from happening in the first place. But that's a topic for a different chapter.

Chapter 11 -- Importance of Keeping Ahead of Hackers

This chapter will focus on staying the course in keeping a step ahead of hackers and cyber-criminals. As with anything else, it's vital to have a plan. You need to form a plan for the defenses of your network and devices and come up with a strategy that allows you to routinely follow through with updates and general checkups on your systems. Otherwise, all of this is pointless. Hopefully, you will keep this material handy for easy reference and it can also serve as those useful reminders to change your passwords and whatnot.

Before we get into specific types of malware, I want to reiterate the importance of keeping up with your antivirus software. By this I mean not simply checking to see if the icon is still on the bottom of the screen. Have it go through some scans every once in awhile. You may even prevent an issue because some piece of malware got lodged in there and hasn't been detected yet, since the software does things on its own schedule. This is possible.

Stay on top of your payment methods. Something as stupid as an expired credit card can all too often occur due to negligence, especially if it's a card you only use for these purposes. Let's face it; there are other things you're understandably more worried about over the course your day. But setting aside a specific time semi-routinely to address these simple tasks can go a long way to preventing the worst case scenario.

Finally, when it's time to renew, don't just automatically do it. Look around. See what's what and ask a few questions. Hopefully you're a lot more educated now than you were before reading this, so you'll have some relevant questions. Most people seem to think IT and security are some sort of alchemy or mysticism, so even if you have a little bit of knowledge, the high priests at the Geek Squad (or wherever you go) will appreciate your effort and be receptive to your concerns.

Forming a plan and staying ahead of the game also fosters the habit of vigilance. At first, you're likely concerned with your business network and the devices within, which is where you should start. After all, safeguarding that information is your responsibility. And as you form a plan and then implement it, suddenly things become familiar and habitual. A mindset is created, and each time you log in or do business over the Internet, you're now making decisions with security in mind.

Also, this will bleed over into your personal life as well. We've discussed how some bad guys can breach through social media, and by staying sharp on the job, you'll suddenly think twice about how much you're sharing with the whole world as opposed to your own little circle. That little voice, the one that probably narrated this book in your head, will question whether you *need* to post this or that. You'll be all the better off for it.

Always keep in mind that once something is posted on the Internet, it's thrown into the cesspool of data that hackers sift through to find a way into your business or personal life. For instance, try Googling your own name. It's terrifying how much is out there. Ask one of your friends to see what they can learn about you from Internet searches and see what they come back with. Then kill them.

You need to be critical of your own habits. Remember that your old way of doing things is either what invited a breach (which possibly is what brought you here) or you realize you're just waiting for a world of inevitable hurt (which brought you here), so start with yourself. This example is simplistic and doesn't apply to most of you, but it's near certain that there are some lads and ladies out there who thinks they're uber smart because they manage to use free Wi-Fi somewhere. While they think they're slick and cutting down on operational costs, they're really showing their backs to the world as they handle payroll business in the middle of a Starbucks with the threat of keyloggers and other forms of evil cyber people who deliberately hang out in places like that for just such an opportunity. Don't be that clown. Evaluate your habits and procedures and be honest with yourself about how vulnerable you really are.

One habit you should definitely cultivate is a regular inspection of your transactions. And I mean really look at those statements. Don't just skim to make sure some moron in Budapest didn't buy a JetSki on your account. There are many small transactions that can appear innocuous but are actually hackers stealing a little bit at a time from a lot of people. It seems harmless, and you may even shrug it off if it's only for a few dollars, but complacency breeds apathy and grows into a huge pain in the neck if you're not staying on top of these things. Hackers depend on you either to overlook their activities altogether or feel too overwhelmed (or embarrassed) to do anything about it. Therefore, they continue to rake in the rewards while their misdeeds go unreported. Stay vigilant and don't be a victim. By making things difficult for them to breach you, you increase the chances that they will move on to easier targets and leave you alone.

Let's go back to your passwords for a minute. Hopefully you've changed all of them (and plan to do so at regular intervals) and ditched the galactically stupid idea of storing them in some vulnerable location in the cloud or as your desktop wallpaper. Now it's time to get a little more serious about this, at least in the initial stages of revamping your security protocols. For instance, install two-step verification for as many accounts as possible. If you've ever had to recover a password and received an email or SMS text with a code, then you understand how this basically works. This might seem extreme at first, but once it's a habit, it won't be that big of a deal and you'll be way ahead of most people.

All of this may seem a little extreme compared to how you're used to operating. But when you consider the fact that massive corporations and folks in the know are changing their behavior based on the kinds of threats that exist out there, it starts to make sense that you should adopt their mindset as well, both for your business and personal networks. Take another cue from these larger entities and tin-foil-donning dorks and study your adversary. Lots of capital is being dumped into research. Governments insist the new frontline is in cyberspace. Why would you not want to be aware of what's going on in this sector? Hackers and their techniques are as diversified as any conglomerate, as they rarely use the same trick too many times in a row. They're constantly adapting. You need to understand this and keep an active understanding if you want to outrun these evolving digital predators.

And like any good plan, there are contingencies. Even with all the greatest preventative measures and best intentions, there is still the possibility you will be breached, which means you need to know how to deal with this ugliness effectively and swiftly in order to mitigate the damage.

The best defense against breaches and hacker schemes is your vigilance in understanding these threats, followed by effective planning. The most important thing to remember is the determination of the cyber-criminal to do their part in the endless struggle between those that presume to steal from those with stuff worth stealing.

And it'll be up to you. While there are advancements in A.I. which can help to discern vulnerabilities as well as hacking capabilities, there is no substitute for the human condition in this case. So while A.I. will sift through the obvious like birthdays and anniversary dates, a hacker is examining your social media presence and identifying possible passwords based on your interests and passions (or whatever it is that you blog about).

Yet even after all these precautions, which you alone are responsible for, it's still wise to call a professional. Speaking of which...

Chapter 12 - Choosing an IT Provider for Cyber Security

Let's assume for the moment that you've decided to hire a professional IT security provider. This is a process in of itself. There's a difference between some kid at the Geek Squad (which may be adequate for your personal device) and a true professional. Here's a hint: The latter is the one you want to look after your enterprise or organization. Take a look around and see who's working on companies with a size similar to yours. Surely you belong to some kind of business community. See what they think.

The need for a security expert goes beyond simply installing and implementing prevention measures. It's also about having someone around who has a better idea than you ever will of what's about to come down the pipe next. We've been hammering home the importance of all this planning, but the truth is, the best plan is to have someone involved in your organization that knows what is happening and what could happen next. Plus, the right people will know precisely what it is that you need for your network. This is why you need to look for a *consultant* as opposed to a mere IT professional. Do you understand the distinction?

Perhaps you don't. The first thing to consider is whether your professional is an innovator or a reactionary. An innovator will examine your situation and tailor your cyber-defense according to your needs and vulnerabilities. They'll examine each piece of your network and discover ways to improve efficiency. They'll remove unnecessary programs and apps that slow things down, improving productivity. They'll have a remote backup storage already set up in the event of a ransomware attack. They'll have a contingency plan in place in the event of a breach, regardless of what kind it may be.

Or you can bring in some guy who simply installs general security measures and waits for the wolf to come to the door.

Ultimately who do you want watching over your network?

Take the time to understand who you're working with and what they are capable of doing. And perhaps most importantly, ask how they are invested in their own continuing education. Cyber security is one of the front lines of technological advancement. You certainly don't want to be relying on any one person or IT firm that considers their game plan to be adequate as-is. You want to work with folks who have a natural and professional urge to know about what's on the horizon and how to combat it.

At the same time, how's their bedside manner? Unfortunately, the IT field is riddled with those who consider themselves to be the high priests, and the prospect of talking to mere mortals about their magic tricks is both disgusting and beyond their ability. Are they impatient with your amateur-hour questions and concerns? Can they effectively communicate the more complicated workings of network protection, threats, and solutions? Remember that you've already adopted the attitude that you *will* be informed in this arena, so your IT professional should meet you halfway and not be a jerk about having to do so.

Naturally, you need to do the due diligence thing. Is this person or firm prepared for their own breaches? (Yes, they have to deal with vulnerabilities, too. They aren't gods, after all.) Do they have backups in place should the inevitable happen, including natural disasters or manmade catastrophes? What is their track record? Again, if you're in a business community, there are probably resources available and recommendations to seek. Coupled with your own research and instincts, find the best cyber-mercenary to make sure your goods remain intact and untouched.

And remember this, too: Simply relying on brand recognition can get you in trouble. For instance, Coca-Cola is popular because they don't mess with the recipe. Their marketing, however, is cutting edge. Does that model belong in the realm of cybersecurity? All those boxes of antivirus software, lined up at the OfficeMax like fancy, artisan boxes of cereal, have been the targets of hackers for years.

So ask questions and get a satisfactory answer that you're in good, innovative hands.

Comodo seems to appear on many companies' list of security providers. For the most part, they offer free and affordable tools such as remote monitoring and management, patch management, and service desk in one place. If you're a small business, you can benefit from antivirus and SSL certificates alongside the Internet security, mobile device management, firewall, and so on.

CloudFare also comes up in many forums and reviews. They are also relatively affordable and have a comparatively unique strategy of staying in front of website and monitoring traffic from that vantage point. This way, your website remains protected from deliberate attacks as well as random visitors phishing or just general mayhem that can shut down a site with Denial of Service (DoS).

If you're looking for a one-stop-shop concept, EST is a viable option. They offer bundles and packages that can protect all manners of devices for both personal and business networks. They work in both Windows and Mac along with their corresponding mobile devices, servers, and emails. One of the more attractive features is your ability to choose which services you need depending on your organization's requirements, which includes two-factor ID, encryption, file security, and other services.

Lookout operates in the mobile protection niche. While computers are always at risk, the rise of mobile devices and their use in business makes them equally vulnerable and susceptible to attack. Lookout Mobile Security attempts exactly what it's name implies -- protection from threats such as malware, data leakage, and sideloaded apps for all mobile devices linked to your business network. Another interesting feature is complete visibility over these devices with advanced tools to watch for risks and deal with them accordingly. They assess these risks, investigate any incidents that occur, and ensure that all compliance or regulatory standards have been met.

These are just a few examples of larger security firms and applications, but there are a lot more out there, and it's up to you to select one that best fits your needs. Should you choose this route, there are some drawbacks. Personalized attention just won't be there. Sure, there will be tech support (and hopefully there will be *someone* to talk to), but that just isn't the same as having your own gunslinger with whom you're on a first name basis.

So another option is smaller firm. Like anything else in the marketplace, there are boutique shops in the cyber-world that cater specifically to smaller businesses. They can be someone you hire as part of your company, assuming you have the means to support your own IT department. You can also enlist a consulting firm that will look after your network systems with a keen eye on the details of what you specifically need. Should you go this route, which admittedly requires more research and due diligence on your part, you'll likely be in safer hands. These are also small businesses in a sense, and they typically conduct themselves with more dedication to their work in order to build and maintain their reputations as safe, reliable, and innovative consultants for IT security.

Let's assume for a moment that you decide to take on a smaller 'boutique' shop. The first thing is finding the right one. That should be obvious -- research, references, and recommendations. Examine your own business and see who's out there with the most experience and satisfaction in dealing with a company like yours in both size and sector. For instance, if you're a medical practice or involved in healthcare in anyway, there's a whole other set of rules and issues you have to contend with on both sides of the law in terms of threats and compliance. In this case, find a security shop that specializes in HIPAA standards and medical data protection.

One way to find and eventually choose the right IT shop is to invite them in for a consultation. Most of them, if they're legitimate, offer some sort of free assessment of your network and will offer their view on how to improve everything from system efficiency to protection. You may even be one of those places that has too many plugs in one surge protector next to a leaking fire suppression system. I'm sure they can offer some tips on that as well.

When you do choose your consultant, be sure to designate one person to serve as a liaison between their team and yours (or you, if you choose to take that role). It does no good to have several people talking to each other about different things, or even about the same thing. It's inefficient and can lead to chaos. Find out what they need to get started and have it ready for them so they can hit the ground running.

Set expectations and goals and make sure all understand them. Be sure to thoroughly document all progress or lack thereof, and keep everyone informed. It's both frustrating and a little awkward when one side is dissatisfied while the other thinks they're kicking tail and taking names.

Finally, have mutually agreed upon terms for renewal or dissolution. After the initial term of service... well... it just might not be a good fit, for whatever reason and from either perspective.

The points above don't really cover all of the red flags and considerations by a long shot, but it should at least give you some idea about choosing how to best protect your business from cyber-crime, among other things. There's a comprehensive checklist we can provide that covers this in greater detail (23 Critical Questions You MUST Ask Before Hiring Any IT Company), and it will better inform you of what to look for and what questions to ask. To request your FREE report, simply email our office at sales@petronellacomputer.com

So that's the sales pitch. Allow us the opportunity to provide a thorough 4-Pillars assessment of your business and, if you're impressed with our professionalism, we can install some measures that will protect you and your organization from any breach - be it minor or catastrophic. We're the only IT professionals that can offer these guarantees -- https://www.petronellacomputer.com/why-petronella/

Four Pillars of IT Success Analysis

The Four Pillars of IT Success: What they are (and why you should care)

There are four main components of a successful IT strategy. These Four Pillars of IT Success, as we call them, are:

1. 100% Uptime
2. Security
3. Applications
4. Collaboration

The Four Pillars of IT Success can make the difference between a business that is efficient and profitable and a business that falls prey to violations (and the expenses that come with it).

Businesses that are small and intend to stay that way can usually get by with what we at Petronella call "break/fix" IT support. However, when you begin to outgrow this impromptu approach to computer care, the costs of dealing with risks and problems as they pop up will eat into profits more and more.

Ignoring the Four Pillars can be especially risky for a company that:

➢ Has 10 or more employees
➢ Utilizes 10 or more computers
➢ Is growing or expanding

If your organization matches this profile, our analysis of your firm's Four Pillars will uncover substantial risks and opportunities hiding within your IT systems.

The Four Pillars analysis is akin to the exams, tests, and consultations you would have with a heart specialist before going in for an actual surgery that could save your life. The analysis is a necessary expense to identify a serious problem so that you can address it and prevent the worst from happening.

And we will improve the health of your bottom line, guaranteed. We will save you a minimum of $100,000 or refund the price of the analysis.

We can confidently offer you this guarantee because we have already seen our Four Pillars approach benefit hundreds of other businesses. Most of the companies that qualify for the Four Pillars Discovery have enjoyed savings of far more than $100,000. One of our clients recently saved $334,000. You can read this client's story—as well as other real-world examples of problems that the Four Pillars Discovery can help you avoid—at the end of this report.

Have You Suffered from These "Break/Fix" Frustrations?

One way to tell whether you would qualify for a Four Pillars analysis (and the $100,000 savings that comes with it) is to ask yourself if you've ever experienced any of the following frustrations.

Frustration #1: Lack of Response from Tech Support
If your network goes down or experiences a serious problem, your entire operation can come to a screeching halt. In today's fast-paced business world, you can't afford to just sit around and wait for your IT specialist to call you back. And you shouldn't be stuck twiddling your thumbs until help arrives to fix the problem. We believe that you should be able to get in contact with someone to correct the problem right away. But even more importantly, we believe your IT specialist should do whatever is necessary to prevent downtime from occurring in the first place.

Frustration #2: Poor Communication and Substandard Service

An all-too-common problem that many business owners have with their IT professionals is poor communication. You should not have to endure arrogant technicians who talk over your head, and you should not be left in the dark about the status of your requests and projects. We believe that strong communication is the foundation of good customer service. Quality communication (or lack thereof) is a primary indicator of whether an IT company is competent enough to organize and manage your computer network.

Frustration #3: Recurring Problems

Every time your IT specialist says that a problem is solved, two more issues rear their ugly heads. To make matters worse, the problems that were supposed to have been solved keep surfacing again and again—and you keep paying to fix them again and again. Your support person justifies the charges by blaming your software, hardware, or some other external issue that they claim cannot be fixed permanently.

If these frustrations sound familiar, we have good news. You most likely qualify for the Four Pillars Discovery, which comes with a guaranteed savings of over $100,000.

Why the Four Pillars?

I'm a firm believer in the Pareto Principle, also known as the 80/20 Rule. It basically says that a small number of fundamental inputs will yield the bulk of our desired outputs. This concept is virtually a universal law, applicable in business, nature, and nearly every other endeavor under the sun.

The Pareto Principle is the reason I designed my discovery and analysis around the Four Pillars. They are the few fundamental inputs that effect massive outputs. This is the most powerful and efficient way to examine your IT challenges and opportunities.

That is why I am so confident that I can identify ways to save over $100,000 for the companies that qualify for the Four Pillars Discovery.

Consider the impact each of the Four Pillars can have when we improve them together:

- ❖ **100% uptime and profitability analysis** – This involves a review of your network strategy, computers, and servers. We take a close, comprehensive look at your hardware, software, and cabling. Even when your IT and network system are of reasonable quality, we can almost always identify five or more factors that can improve uptime and profitability. Of these five factors, two or three are likely to have a substantial impact on your top and bottom lines.

- ❖ **Security audit, in layers, beginning with your perimeter or firewall protection** – Without adequate firewall protection, you can find yourself the victim of viruses, hacking, ransomware, or even identity theft. We inspect your entire network infrastructure to ensure that security updates and performance patches are as they should be.

- ❖ **Applications appraisal** – We perform a systematic review of your business applications, studying your workflow to find areas that could be improved with alternative software packages, cloud computing applications, or more efficient processes.

- ❖ **Collaboration** – We pay close attention to your unique methods of working with your team and vendors. An accurate understanding of your business needs allows us to tailor our recommendations, streamline your operations, facilitate growth of your business, and increase your profits.

In short, the Four Pillars are all about leverage—giving you the biggest bang for your IT buck.

Consider these examples, just a few of the high-leverage factors we will assess during the analysis:

1. **Maintenance of computers and servers** – Software updates come out weekly, and the majority of small businesses think that these updates are unnecessary. Not so. Neglected software eventually leads to downtime and technology failure. Without patches, hackers can get ahead of you. Without regular cleaning and maintenance, computers and servers will overheat. Skipping the upkeep of your network backbone equipment makes it vulnerable to overheating and external attacks. Hard drives and servers gradually fill up and run out of space. If you don't perform maintenance, you're going to crash.

   Example: Install the latest version of Java on all your systems to protect your company from the latest hacker threat. Your server hosts everything for your practice, so if that server goes down, employees can't access client files and other information necessary to do their jobs. This loss of productivity costs your practice the hourly salary multiplied by the number of employees.

2. **Data backup and disaster recovery** – Many companies believe they have a good system, but their audit reveals otherwise. If you were to suffer a failure, or if your building burned down today, would you be able to recover? One woman had 30,000 pictures of her kids, family, friends, vacations, and other cherished moments she'd collected over the years. If she experienced a crash, all of those irreplaceable mementos would be lost forever. What memories and other important documents might you lose in a crash?

3. **Security** – Inadequate firewall protection. Viruses. Missed security updates and performance patches. Through network monitoring, it is possible to proactively detect and thwart impending failure and downtime. Don't leave yourself open to virus infections, hacking, and slow performance.

4. **Wiring** – Faulty or incorrect wiring can cause a network to go down.

5. **Power protection** – Only 20% of businesses have proper power protection. There are nine major power problems, any of which risks harming your computers and corrupting your data. If a critical operating system file were to be corrupted, your entire system would no longer boot properly, leading to a crash. This means downtime and setbacks for your staff. Does your server have a dedicated power outlet? Protect yourself from all nine major power problems.

   > **Example:** The server shares an electrical circuit with a copier. The copier triggers an unexpected shutdown, and important files that ten employees were collaborating on are forever lost. The most recent data backup was last night at midnight, so all progress made since then is gone.

6. **Opportunities** – Cloud computing could potentially cut your IT service expenses in half.

Most companies with ten or more employees can save $100,000 in just five years. This is often the equivalent of increasing gross revenue sales by $1,000,000. But the savings won't stop there. The Four Pillars will affect continuous savings that increase your bottom line year after year.

As part of the Four Pillars Discovery analysis, we will:

✓ Identify any warning signs in your current IT environment.

✓ Map out a solution to address existing threats.

✓ Provide an IT action plan to help your practice reach goals and eliminate problems before they escalate into disasters.

✓ Diagnose chronic problems or concerns that have plagued the computers on your network.

✓ Scan for hidden viruses, spyware, and loopholes in your network security that could open the door for hackers and cybercriminals to access confidential healthcare information.

✓ Check your system backups for corruption and recoverability in case of an emergency.

✓ Review your network configuration and peripheral devices to maximize performance and speed.

✓ Search server file logs for impending problems or conflicts that can cause unexpected downtime.

✓ Ensure that all security updates and patches are current.

Our goal is simplicity. Just a handful of significant actions can reward you with significant growth to your bottom line. We don't focus on trivialities. We focus on results. If we don't find $100,000 worth of improvements to your bottom line, we will issue a full refund for the Four Pillars Discovery.

See the end of this report for true case studies of the dangers of ignoring the Four Pillars.

What Does It Cost?

The amount of investment for the Four Pillars Discovery is figured individually for each business or medical practice. Your servers, software, IT infrastructure, and number of employees are all factors. Rest assured that this is a worthwhile expenditure. We guarantee that we will save you $100,000 or we'll completely refund your money. Call Craig Petronella at (919) 601-1601 to review your options today!

Your customized Four Pillars report will include:

- ➤ Analysis of how your practice measures up to HIPAA and industry norms in all Four Pillars areas

- ➤ The three largest risks to your systems and how to address these risks

- ➤ The three greatest opportunities for you to boost productivity and profits

- ➤ A clear, simple, customized IT success plan to achieve HIPAA compliance and reach industry standards in all Four Pillar areas

What can you expect from your Four Pillars IT success plan?

- ➤ Elimination of all ticking IT time bombs, guaranteeing HIPAA compliance

- ➤ Total protection from viruses, worms, and malware on your network

- ➤ Insight into how your practice can take advantage of secure cloud solutions

- ➤ A review of Section 179 opportunities that could potentially reduce your taxes

Based on real-world results, medical offices that qualify for the Four Pillars Discovery can expect a reduction of at least 50% in their IT service expenses. That benefit is in addition to the $100,000 of savings you can enjoy over the next one to five years, not to mention the frustration you avoid by eliminating downtime and system failures.

For real examples of the impact of the Four Pillars, see the client stories at the end of this report.

What Happens After The Four Pillars Analysis?

When the Four Pillars analysis is complete, we will sit down with you to go over our findings and the implications. At that point, you will decide on an option of how to proceed:

1. You design and implement our recommendations yourself.

2. You hire us to design and implement the recommendations. If you have us start within two weeks of our analysis, I will credit the cost of the Four Pillars Discovery toward the cost of implementation.

3. If we don't find $100,000 of savings for you (highly unlikely) OR if you find no value in the Four Pillars Discovery, I will issue a full refund. This is an **unconditional GUARANTEE.**

Your Next Step

Call Craig Petronella at (919) 601-1601 to review your options and get started today!

Actual Disasters the Four Pillars Could (or Did) Prevent

These folks learned the importance of the Four Pillars. Some of them learned the hard way.

The $40,000 Ticking Time Bomb

Tick. Tick. Tick.

It started as a little clicking noise. A tad annoying, yes, but fairly easy to ignore. Especially since it was only on one computer.

Tock. Tock. Tock.

Joe, the owner of the company, had no clue what the clicking sound was. And because there were always bigger fires to put out and more pressing projects to keep him busy, Joe's part-time IT specialist already had a plate full of things that didn't tick. The mysterious noise went unchecked.

Tick. Tock. BOOM!

Just like that, the hard drive was toast. All server information was destroyed. As it turns out, the ticking was the sound of avoidable IT expenses, creeping up dollar by dollar.

The problem could have easily been avoided with the Four Pillars diagnostic and analysis tools.

Instead...

$12,500 for repairs
$27,500 for lost productivity

$40,000 total preventable expense

The Virus with the $20,000 Cure

A local auto body shop came to realize that they weren't experts on every kind of crash.

The owner's brother gave him part-time IT support, running around to the multiple shop locations and dealing with individual computer issues as they arose. Preventative maintenance was not part of the equation, but everything seemed to be going fine anyway.

That changed when one of the employees clicked on a link she thought had come from a friend. A virus infected her PC and inundated her with uncontrollable popups. Her CPU spiked to 100%, and she couldn't run any commands or programs. When she shut down the computer and rebooted, it wouldn't even load into the operating system. Thankfully, the virus was limited to the one computer.

Except that it wasn't.

The nasty little bug replicated, attached itself to files, and spread. It wasn't long before the virus:

> - Corrupted their data and made important files completely inaccessible to a staff of 50
> - Impaired their customer management system, making it a nightmare to open simple records
> - Brought down their Exchange server so that sending and receiving email was impossible

Total business meltdown. One simple click on a seemingly harmless link threw them back to 1985—dependent on telephone calls and paper forms.

Skipping the ounce of prevention doomed them to pay for the pound of cure. It cost them $20,000 to remove the virus, restore their network, and get things running properly again.

And all that the $20,000 did was get them back to where they started. Their systems were not optimized to prevent something similar from happening again. They were merely back to square one, and still vulnerable to the same type of attack in the future.

The Four Pillars Discovery would have made them immune to that virus.

A Healthcare Business Makes a Healthy Choice

A diagnostic we performed on a healthcare company's systems revealed that they were at risk for a disaster like the one that befell the auto body shop.

We fixed the problem.

A shorter story, yes, but with a much happier ending. And that's the point.

Another Healthcare Company Saves $344,672.00

This company signed on as a new client in March of 2012, when they moved their operations from Florida to North Carolina. The relocation came with a staff reduction. They no longer needed as many computers as they had.

Their total cost was $50,000, and the money they are saving on technology and IT support as a result of our analysis comes to $344,672.00 (plus maintenance and lease) over a period of five years.

This Company in the Automotive Industry Avoids Costly Downtime

Although this client had a reasonably good IT system, they were not adequately protected from the nine power problems. During our analysis, we identified ten factors with the potential to cause costly downtime. We also revealed holes in their network that were putting them at great risk for infection by viruses.

They hired me to make the improvements necessary to achieve 100% uptime. We are also maintaining their system with proactive managed services, as well as building a robust and efficient pipeline that will remove their virus risk.

And we are doing all of this while saving them a significant amount of money.

Construction Business Lays a Solid IT Foundation

One of our many clients in the construction industry hired us in 2002 to maintain their network. During our analysis, we discovered seven issues that were just waiting for the right moment (wrong moment, really) to cause downtime.

In addition to these problems, which we solved, we also put into place a cloud computing solution that would save the business more than $215,000 in just five years.

We continue to proactively monitor and maintain the client's network 24/7. They have never suffered a server meltdown on our watch, and we intend to keep it that way.

Find out if your company is eligible for similar savings. Contact me today.
Phone: (919) 601-1601
Email: Craig@PetronellaComputer.com

Appendix

A key to the acronyms and other terms used in this book:

BA – Business Associate – An organization that manages, transmits, modifies, or otherwise handles PHI and is therefore responsible for adhering to HIPAA standards

CE – Covered Entity – An organization that creates and originates PHI and is therefore directly responsible for adhering to HIPAA standards

DFARS – Defense Federal Acquisition Regulation Supplement – A supplement used by the Department of Defense to ensure security when working with contractors

ePHI – Electronic Personal Health Information – PHI in electronic format

FACTA – Fair and Accurate Credit Transactions Act – An amendment to the Fair Credit Reporting Act that allows consumers free access to annual credit reports, contains provisions to reduce identity theft, and requires secure disposal of consumer information.

GLBA – Gramm-Leach-Bliley Act – Requires financial institutions to explain their information-sharing practices to customers and to protect sensitive data

HHS – Department of Health and Human Services – The organization responsible for upholding HIPAA compliance

HIPAA – Health Insurance Portability and Accountability Act –

Legislation to improve, among other things, the security of an individual's private health information

HITECH – Health Information Technology for Economic and Clinical Health Act – Legislation that, among other things, governs the handling of patient information in electronic form and promotes adoption of information technology for use in the medical field

ISO 27001 – An international standard of security, compliance with which is required to do business with various customers and associates, including entities in the government and medical industry

NIST 800-171 – A set of expectations that align with U.S. government security controls that all contractors must satisfy in order to do business with the government

OCR – Office of Civil Rights – The division of the HHS that enforces HIPAA rules and performs audits to check for compliance

PCI-DSS – The Payment Card Industry Data Security Standard – An information security standard for organizations that handle major branded credit cards. Created and compliance-checked by the card brands, it increases controls around cardholder data to reduce credit card fraud.

PHI – Personal Health Information (or Protected Health Information) – Any information that directly connects an individual to a specific health condition

SOC – Service Organization Controls – A set of standards and guidelines to be used by auditors of IT systems when evaluating security compliance

SOX – Sarbanes-Oxley Act – A U.S. federal law that set new and expanded requirements for public company boards, management, and public accounting firms to protect shareholders and the general public from accounting errors and fraudulent practices

ZDP – Zero Day Plus – International reseller of patented security that stops all zero-day malware and ransomware proactively by preventing the offending program from writing to a computer's hard drive.

www.ingramcontent.com/pod-product-compliance
Lightning Source LLC
Chambersburg PA
CBHW070845070326
40690CB00009B/1710